D0643348

THE
BIGGEST
GAME
· IN ·
TOWN

By A. Alvarez

GENERAL

Under Pressure

The Savage God:
A Study of Suicide

Life After Marriage:
Love in an Age of Divorce

The Biggest Game in Town

NOVELS

Hers

Hunt

CRITICISM

Stewards of Excellence

The School of Donne

Beyond All This Fiddle

Samuel Beckett

POETRY

Lost

Apparition

Penguin Modern Poets No. 18

Autumn to Autumn,
and Selected Poems 1953–76

ANTHOLOGY

The New Poetry
(Editor, and Introduction by)

A. ALVAREZ

THE BIGGEST GAME · IN · TOWN

Boston

HOUGHTON MIFFLIN COMPANY

1983

LIBRARY

JUN 7 1984

UNIVERSITY OF THE PACIFIC

Western
Americana 418639

HV
6721
L3
A45
1983

The contents of this book originally appeared,
in slightly different form, in *The New Yorker*.

Copyright © 1983 by A. Alvarez

All rights reserved. No part of this work may be reproduced
or transmitted in any form or by any means, electronic or
mechanical, including photocopying and recording, or by
any information storage or retrieval system, except as
may be expressly permitted by the 1976 Copyright Act or in
writing from the publisher. Requests for permission should
be addressed in writing to Houghton Mifflin Company,
2 Park Street, Boston, Massachusetts 02108.

Library of Congress Cataloging in Publication Data

Alvarez, A. (Alfred), date
The biggest game in town.

"Contents: . . . originally appeared, in slightly
different form, in the New Yorker"—T.p. verso.
Includes index.
1. Gambling—Nevada—Las Vegas.   2. Poker.
3. Gamblers—United States—Biography.   I. Title.
HV6721.L3A45   1983   795.41′2′0979313   82–23415
ISBN 0–395–33964–2

Printed in the United States of America

D 10 9 8 7 6 5 4 3 2 1

To David and Jane Cornwell

1

NINE o'clock on a Tuesday morning at the end
of April 1981, and according to the giant illuminated
figures at the top of the Mint Hotel the temperature was
already ninety-two degrees. At the entrance of Binion's
Horseshoe Casino stood the famous horseshoe itself,
seven feet high, painted gold, and enclosing within its
arch a million dollars in ten-thousand-dollar bills. The
hundred bills are neatly ranked and held, for whatever
foreseeable eternity, in some kind of super-perspex —
bulletproof, fireproof, bombproof — the perennial dream
of the Las Vegas punter visible to all, although not quite
touchable. If you come too close, one of Binion's giant
security guards, leather straps polished and creaking over

his beige uniform, gun in his holster, moves quietly forward.

The million-dollar horseshoe reflected the glare of the morning sun on Fremont Street. Behind it were gloom and movement: a long, low, rather shabby room, full of noise and smoke, and, unlike the other casinos at this early hour, full of people. Women in halters and men in cowboy boots and Stetsons jostled each other around the roulette and craps tables, rattled the armies of slot machines, and perched in semicircles before the blackjack dealers; even the seats in the little keno lounge were mostly taken. At the back, there was already a crowd along the rail that separates the casual punters from the area that, for five weeks every year in the last decade, has been set aside for poker.

Fixed to one wall of this makeshift poker room was a large yellow banner, announcing in red, BINION'S HORSE-SHOE PRESENTS THE WORLD SERIES OF POKER 1981. Opposite was an equally large blackboard, listing across the top the side games being played that day while the official tournament was in progress: "Hold 'Em, No Limit — 5, 10, 25," "Hold 'Em, No Limit — 25, 25, 50," "7 STUD — 50, 100," "7 STUD — 200, 400." Under each set of figures was a column of names and initials. The larger the numbers, the shorter the column beneath.

The game just inside the rail seemed to have been going on all night. The players were gray-faced and un-shaven. They shifted about uncomfortably in their seats, yawned, scratched vaguely at their grubby shirts, lit one cigarette from the stub of another. They looked, most of them, like the uneasy sleepers on the benches in railway stations, sitting there because they could not raise the price of a hotel room. Only the dealer seemed dressed for the occasion: he wore a gleaming white shirt and a narrow black bow tie with two long tails, Western style, inscribed with the word *Horseshoe*. He checked the bets in front of the three players who remained in the pot, and raked those chips into the pile of chips at the center of the table; then he discarded the top card of the deck he held, and turned over a communal card, to join four already exposed in front of him. A cowboy to his left tapped twice on the table with his forefinger. To the cowboy's left, an elderly man in a bulging T-shirt stared meditatively at the exposed cards, took two black chips from the stack in front of him, and tossed them toward the center. He seemed utterly uninterested, as if the matter were somehow beneath his attention. "Two dollars," said the dealer, in a bored voice. The next player, a nervous young man with a Zapata mustache, cupped his hands around two cards face down in front of him, squeezed up their corners, and flicked them toward the dealer, elegantly, like a fop making a conversational point. Only the cowboy was left. He tilted his Stetson back an inch and stared at the elderly man, unblinking, for a full minute. While he stared, he juggled a pile of black chips up and down on the baize in front of him — up and down, in and out, like a yo-yo on a string. His fingers were agile and surprisingly long. Then his hand stopped abruptly, he lifted seven chips off the pile without seeming to count them, and he pushed them into the center. "Raise it up a nickel," he said. The fat elderly man crossed his arms on his chest, sank his chin toward them, and considered the cowboy. There was a long pause. In the same bored voice, the dealer said, "Five dollars to you."

A nickel? Five dollars? This was my first morning in Las Vegas, so I leaned forward to see the markings on

3

the black chips. In the middle of each was a white disc decorated with the casino's symbol, around which was printed "Horseshoe Club, Las Vegas, Nev." Inside the horseshoe was a portrait of the owner, Benny Binion, in a cowboy hat, smiling encouragingly over his signature. Below that was the figure "$100." So now I knew. Later, I was told that serious gamblers always leave off the zeros when they announce bets. Perhaps it is a way of showing their indifference. The bigger the bet, the more zeros omitted. In gambling parlance, a nickel is $500, a dime is $1000, a big dime is $10,000. "It makes it simpler," I was told. It also makes it more unreal.

Unreal. Over in the back corner of the enclosure, as far from the spectators as they could decently manage, another group of men was settling down to a new game. Their clothes were pressed, their hair was brushed, and they moved in an aura of after-shave and talcum powder. I recognized some of the faces from newspaper photographs and from pictures in Doyle Brunson's book *Super/System,* a large treatise on advanced poker techniques, strictly for postgraduates. I had studied the book like a Biblical scholar before I left London, but now I found, to my irritation, that I could remember the faces more vividly than I could remember the advice and the card analysis. Brunson himself was at the table, and Bobby Baldwin and Puggy Pearson, all of them winners, in their turn, of the World Series Poker Championship, and there were several others, some of whose faces I vaguely recognized but whose names I could not place. The big league was settling down to a morning's entertainment. The men chatted while they nonchalantly unloaded their racks of chips and arranged them at their places at the table: massed towers of black, a couple of towers of gray five-hundred-dollar chips, and then, as an afterthought, a lower bastion of green twenty-five-dollar chips. Each player seemed to have his own architectural plan in mind, but the final effect was of so many grim desert fortresses. Then they fumbled around in their trouser pockets and pulled out packets of money, which they set between the chips and the raised leather edge of the table, like the garrison that the fortifications were protecting. The packets were of hundred-dollar bills, as freshly laundered as the players, and each was belted with a paper band on which was printed "5000 DOLLARS." It was a quarter past nine on a weekday morning, and the boys were settling down for a quiet game of cards.

Welcome to Dreamland.

* * *

But England at the end of that April seemed no more real. That was the coldest spring of the century. Gales hammered the coastline, and the hills were drifted over by snow deep enough to kill newly dropped lambs by the thousand. The day before I left, a party of teen-agers had died of exposure on Dartmoor, and the roads in the gentle southwest were impassable. In normal years, England has no weather to speak of: soggy winters, chilly summers, a dank and penitential mediocrity, with remissions for good behavior. But that year even the climate seemed to be conspiring to demoralize the place: recession, inflation, mass unemployment, strikes, riots, and now blizzards. The mild nation of gardeners and dog lovers seemed to have faded into some remote historical past, along with "Aprille with his shoures soote."

Since there were stoppages, as usual, at all the airports, I called Gatwick to inquire about my flight. It took me an hour to get through. In a toneless and official voice, the operator said, "Passengers are requested to check in two hours before departure time."

"Why two hours?"

There was a pause. Then she gave up. "Because it's such a bloody mess here." She was still giggling when she hung up.

The chaos had subsided by late afternoon, and the airport was peaceful, but we waited half an hour for clearance out on the tarmac, the engines whistling into the icy Sussex hedgerows. Later, in the breaks between clouds, England was like Scandinavia — snow wherever you looked. But by then another reality had begun. It was Western Airlines' second direct flight from London to Las Vegas, and everyone was enthusiastic, eager to please, vaguely celebratory. British chill dissolved in the taste of bourbon and the broad, lazy accents of the stewardesses as we flew westward through the endlessly prolonged twilight.

We cleared customs at Denver, and after that the huge plane was almost empty. So was McCarran Airport when we landed, soon after midnight. So was the town itself, since this was a Tuesday morning and the weekend rush was over. I shared a taxi with an English lawyer who was in town for a week to make a deal. It was his first visit, he told me, and he added glumly, "I don't really gamble, but I suppose I will."

Downtown, where Binion's Horseshoe, the Golden Nugget, the Fremont, and the Four Queens face one another at the intersection of Fremont Street and Casino Center, the blaze of lights was like a steel furnace. The lawyer winced, and said, "We haven't got anything like this in London." But he, too, seemed to have been softened by the friendliness of the airline and a night temperature hotter than the hottest English summer; the tone of his voice was puzzled, awestruck, but not at all disapproving.

"Ain't nothing like it anywhere," said the bearded cabdriver.

"Ain't nothing like it anywhere." Not yet. Perhaps the moon will be like Vegas when the mining colonies are set up, blazing under their transparent domes. Instead of a giant bell jar, Vegas has air conditioning. Twenty-five miles away, the Hoover Dam pumps out the millions of kilowatts without which the whole enterprise would collapse, eroded by the intolerable heat, and be handed back to the Paiute Indians, the leathery prospectors, and the Mormons, who were the first white men to settle here. But now the air conditioning and the desert work together to keep the gambling economy running: at high noon, it is too hot for golf or tennis, or even swimming; the casinos are the only alternative. Perhaps the whole of the new Sun Belt culture thrives in the same way: its population, shuttling in air-conditioned cars between air-conditioned homes and air-conditioned offices and factories, is kept artificially cool, artificially vigorous in the teeth of a debilitating nature — a culture of the future, defined by technology and dependent on it.

Las Vegas is the logical conclusion of what is for the foreigner one of the eeriest aspects of America: the utter lack of continuity between the large towns and their surrounding countryside. They used to say you could walk across London on the grass, and though that was not strictly true, it was not altogether crazy. The greenness of the European countryside penetrates the cities, and the influence of the cities spreads outward, beyond the suburbs, to and fro, in a continual back-and-forth seepage,

7

domesticating and subduing the landscape. From Stockholm to the Mediterranean, there seems to be nowhere that someone has not set foot before you.

In America, this subtle connection scarcely exists. Big cities like New York and Chicago are their own manmade landscapes, endless and self-contained, so that, walking their streets, you find it impossible even to imagine another way of life. Yet within an hour, across the Hudson and off the turnpike, there are deer and skunk in the woods, giving you a sense not of countryside but of the original wilderness. In Denver years ago, before it began to boom, I turned a corner in the honky-tonk downtown and saw the Rockies framed at the end of a long perspective of neon signs, and thought I was hallucinating. It was like peering up Broadway from Times Square and seeing Everest. American cities look inward at themselves, as if the land beyond them were too inhospitable to be contemplated.

The farther west you travel, the greater the sense of wilderness and inhospitality. The tawny deserts of New Mexico and Arizona, quivering in the heat and lunar blue at the horizon, are heartbreakingly beautiful and also heartbreakingly indifferent to the efforts of those who try to make a life in them, despite them. J. B. Priestley once remarked that in the Southwest you are more aware of geology than of history. The land is too big, too old, too parched, too obdurate; the only alternative to submission is defiance, like Brigham Young's institutional Gothic in Salt Lake City, rising like St. Pancras Station from the sandstone and bitter salt flats of Utah.

It was Brigham Young who sent the first white settlers to Las Vegas, in 1855. But it was almost a hundred years before the town had its own wild, science-fiction version

8

of institutional Gothic. Las Vegas was officially founded on May 15, 1905, at a land auction by the San Pedro, Los Angeles & Salt Lake Railroad Company, but began to flourish only after the state of Nevada legalized gambling, in 1931. At first, there was just a handful of shabby gaming saloons at what is now the downtown crossroads. For genuine action and glitter, 1930s gamblers went to Reno, which, as a ranch town, had a certain substance and identity apart from gambling. But in 1939 the federal government started to build the Hoover Dam in Boulder City, and Las Vegas was the nearest place of any size where the construction workers could gamble their money away. What Boulder City began, Los Angeles, less than six hours' drive across the blinding Mojave Desert, continued. As is proper for a gambling town, Las Vegas got lucky — geographically lucky. Its permanent population is now well over half a million and rising.

In its present form, the town, like Andrew Marvell's love, was "begotten by despair upon impossibility." To be precise, it was begotten by an East Coast hit man turned warlord upon the alkali-and-mesquite wastes beyond the city limits. In 1937, the late Benjamin Siegel — known commonly, though never to his face, as Bugsy — left New Jersey for Hollywood with the vague idea of becoming an actor (he was a friend of George Raft) and also with a syndicate commission to lean on the studios and take control of the racing wire to the West Coast. He did not become an actor, but he did tie up the racing wire, and in the process visited Las Vegas often: came, saw, and worked out the odds. What he saw was the opportunity for a giant casino outside town on the Los Angeles road, to catch the tourists on their way in. So in 1945 he built the Flamingo — huge, plush, and festooned from top to bottom with lights, as though defying anyone to pass it by. He thought of it as a monument to himself, and he was right, although not quite in the way he intended. In its first couple of years, the Flamingo defied all the known odds of gambling and lost money consistently. An unlucky streak, Siegel complained, but his backers were not amused. They were even less amused by his refusal to surrender the West Coast racing wire to the national syndicate. On June 20, 1947, Bugsy Siegel was shot to death in Beverly Hills, at 808 North Linden Drive — the house he had bought for his mistress, Virginia Hill. Three days before, Miss Hill herself had conveniently left for a holiday in France. In Las Vegas, Siegel's memory is still revered. The Flamingo was a kind of Rubik's Cube of the postwar years — the big bright idea that others could profit from. Casino followed casino, and the road west out of town became the Strip. It now stretches for six miles into the Clark County desert, palace after palace, outlandish gesture after outlandish gesture.

The casinos lie out there on the baked earth like extravagant toys discarded on a beach, their signs looping, beckoning, spiraling, and fizzing recklessly, as in that moment of glory just before the batteries run down. "Las Vegas," wrote Tom Wolfe, "is the only town in the world whose skyline is made up neither of buildings, like New York, nor of trees, like Wilbraham, Massachusetts, but signs. One can look at Las Vegas from a mile away on Route 91 and see no buildings, no trees, only signs." But what the signs are signaling so hectically are invitations less to luck than to fantasy. The Strip is a Disneyland for the middle-aged, its hotels conceived not just as places to stay but as Hollywood sets, each built round an idea, each offering its guests the chance to star in the movie of their choice. Those who have secretly hankered after *Ben Hur* go to Caesars Palace, where they can lounge on Cleopatra's Barge (with a view of the gaming tables) while their drinks are served by girls dressed as Roman slaves. At Aladdin's, it's *The Arabian Nights,* at the Dunes and the Sahara discrete versions of *The Desert Song,* and at Circus-Circus *Big Top,* with trapeze artists flying about above your head while you gamble and a gallery of battering sideshows to bemuse the children. Each is a world in itself, staffed by upward of three thousand people, with its own swimming pool, gymnasium, and arcade of expensive shops; many of the hotels have tennis courts or golf courses, and most of them stage elaborate supper shows, with famous stars and full supporting casts, more lavish and expensively staged than Broadway musicals. Together, they constitute a kind of movieland version of the Borscht Belt, with gambling as an added element of fantasy and release. They also offer anyone with even a modest bankroll an appearance of the opulence, luxury, and obsequious service that is elsewhere reserved for the very rich. For the few days his money lasts, the Las Vegas tourist can in every possible way feel like a film star.

The typical guest at a Strip hotel is middle-aged and middle class — over a quarter of the guests are college graduates, a fifth are self-employed — and that is how the casinos want it. They are more interested in turnover than in the really high rollers. This is why they have failed to attract the oil-rich Arabs who fuel the gambling economy of Europe. The Arabs, I was told, find Las Vegas rules too restrictive. If they bet the table limit on a single number at roulette, they are not allowed to double that bet on a split number, or treble or quadruple it on a three-way or four-way chance, as they can in London. The conglomerates that now own most of the casinos do not want million-dollar winners, or even million-dollar losers. They want steadier, more moderate customers — those who will win or lose tens of thousands of dollars at most. Which is, of course, more than enough to wipe out the majority of us. But in the world of really big-time gambling they order these things differently, and Las Vegas has lost out as a result. Its casinos turn over more than a billion dollars a year, but democratically, from twelve million weekenders, conventioneers, and passing tourists and some sixty thousand couples served annually by the town's second industry — quick marriages.

There are two exceptions to this rule, and they converge every year in the late spring. Las Vegas has the highest, hardest poker games in the world, twenty-four hours a day, seven days a week, fifty-two weeks a year. It also has Binion's Horseshoe — the one casino where none of the limit rules apply. The gambler at the Horseshoe is allowed to set his own limit with his first bet. In 1980, for example, someone drove in off the desert carrying two suitcases, one empty, the other containing $777,000 in hundred-dollar bills. He took the suitcases to the cage at the back of the casino and changed the neat packets of money into chips, and then, escorted by security guards, he carried his racked chips to a craps table, bet the lot on a single throw of the dice, won, returned to the cage with his double load of chips, filled both his suitcases with money, and drove away. His only comment was "I reckoned inflation was going to eat that money up anyway, so I might as well double it or lose it all." He has not been back.

It could have happened nowhere in Las Vegas except at Binion's. The big casinos on the Strip, despite their apparent opulence and glamour, would not even have considered a bet of that size, because the men who run them are merely employees of business organizations with their offices elsewhere. The Horseshoe, however, is a family concern, which was founded by Benny Binion and is run by him and his two sons, Jack and Teddy. One or another of them is always there when a decision has to be made. Jack Binion, a fit-looking man in his forties, with not much hair and with a seemingly innocent country face — round eyes, large mouth, snub nose, ears like jug handles — spoke of their no-limit policy rather formally, as though it were a question of business philosophy: "One of the problems of American commerce today is that corporations have ceased to be product-oriented and have become financial institutions. Because of mergers and inflation, the financial men have taken over the country and the corporations. Business structures have changed, because that's where the profit is. I would guess that eighty percent of the top five hundred corporations are run by investment-banker types who have come in from the financial side instead of working their way up through the ranks. Very few production men are heads of corporations today. But I think the atmosphere is changing, and in ten years the line men will be back in charge."

But perhaps this was no more than an elaborate way of rationalizing a personal taste and a personal style, since the Binions themselves are gamblers and the high rollers who come to the Horseshoe are mostly their friends. The Binions have played cards with them, or golf or tennis; they have even staked some of them when they were broke. "In the gambling world, your social life and your business life become so interrelated that they are one and the same," Jack said. The gamblers themselves put it more strongly. "For the serious player, the Binions *are* gambling in Vegas," I was told. The professional poker players I spoke to were unanimous only in their attitude toward the Binion family: not just admiration but — an even rarer feeling in that edgy and exclusive world — affection. That attitude permeates the casino itself — shabby, ill-lit, and crowded at all hours. "We're small," said Jack Binion. "Therefore, everyone is jammed together. But people are having a good time, and that gives the place an atmosphere of its own. We've been here a long time, and I like to think of us as a gamblers' gambling house. Not that the other places are just catering to tourists, but the guy who comes here is the sophisticated player. We're like a discount house: no frills, a kind of self-service, but you get the best deals."

That down-home, family atmosphere would not be possible among the grisly Hollywood-style palaces of the Strip, nor would it be appropriate. The Horseshoe belongs to downtown Las Vegas, a geographically separate entity, otherwise known as Glitter Gulch — eight dollars by taxi from Caesars or twenty minutes by bus — to which the punters are ferried in from Los Angeles by the coachload, like migrant workers to the California fruit farms, and where the hotels have no tennis courts or golf courses or gymnasiums, and only a couple of them have swimming pools (smaller than average back-yard pools in suburban Phoenix) tucked away on their roofs. Downtown Las Vegas is strictly for gambling; there is nothing else to do, nowhere else to go. Fremont Street is lined with shops peddling cheap clothes and hideous souvenirs and zircon rings and pornography. In an area of about four blocks, there are more pawnshops than in the whole of Greater London. But I discovered only one drugstore, one five-and-ten, and nowhere at all to buy groceries or fruit. Ordinary shops are banished, like ordinary life, to the shopping centers and the suburbs.

Glitter Gulch is for transients, most of them elderly and dressed to kill: old women in lime green or banana yellow or Florida orange pants suits, clutching Dixie cups of small change in one hand, the lever of one of Vegas's fifty thousand slot machines in the other; old men with plastic teeth and sky blue plastic suits shooting craps for a dollar, playing fifty-cent blackjack and three-dollar-limit stud poker; wrecks in wheelchairs or with walking frames, the humped, the bent, the skeleton thin, and the obese, cashing in their Social Security checks, disability allowances, and pensions, waiting out their time in the hope of a miracle jackpot to transform their last pinched days. All of them are animated by a terrible Walpurgisnacht jollity, gamblers' optimism compounded by nostalgia. THE GOOD OLD DAYS, say the neon signs, and 50¢ BAR DRINKS, WIN A CAR 25¢, FREE ASPIRIN & TENDER SYMPATHY. For the Snopeses of this world, Glitter Gulch is the absurd last stop on the slow train to the grave.

The young are fewer and not much more presentable. The trim, straight-backed young people who roam with such extraordinary grace and confidence around the rest of the United States and seem to be America's most triumphant export to Europe have mostly bypassed downtown Vegas. Instead, the rule for both sexes is big bottoms, beer bellies, and skin muddied by Big Macs and French fries. The boys have tattoos on their arms, and the girls' heads are permed and dyed so relentlessly that a natural head of hair seems like a visitation; you stare after it, thinking, who is *that*?

None of them, young or old, are any more awful than

the tourists on the Strip; they are simply less obviously affluent and considerably more single-minded. For Glitter Gulch is where the real action is, the thing in itself, with no pretensions to glamour or luxury, or even holiday making. The people are there simply to gamble, and most of them, sooner or later, try their luck at the Horseshoe. It is the natural setting for the World Series of Poker.

2

$\mathbb{B}$ENNY BINION is now seventy-seven years old, a genial, round-faced, round-bellied man, like a beardless Santa Claus in a Stetson, benign and smiling. Yet when he left Texas, thirty-five years ago, his police record included bootlegging, gambling, theft, carrying concealed weapons, and two murder charges. (One was dismissed as "self-defense," and for the other he was given a suspended two-year sentence.) Like his contemporary and long-time friend Johnny Moss, three times World Poker Champion, Benny came from a dirt-poor family — his father was a stockman — and made his fortune the hard way, by his wits, starting as a "hip-pocket bootlegger." Moss explained to me, "He kept his stuff in a stash car round downtown Dallas. He'd go get a pint, put it in his hip pocket, sell it, and go get another pint." After the repeal of Prohibition, he moved into gambling, which was then, as it is now, illegal in the state of Texas. By the time the Second World War ended, he had become "kind of the boss of gambling down there in Dallas," his son Jack said. He left town precipitately in 1946. "I had to get out," he is reported to have said. "My sheriff got beat in the election that year." So he moved to Las Vegas, where gambling was legal, and eventually bought the Horseshoe, a shabby little casino that had begun life in 1937 as the El Dorado Club. As for the illegalities in his past, he says, "Tough times make tough people."

In 1953, the tough times caught up with him again: he was sentenced to five years in the federal penitentiary at Leavenworth for income tax evasion. The casino was sold to a man from New Orleans, and the Binion clan did not regain complete control of it until 1964. Even then, the law was not finished with Benny, although he had become, I was told, the third most powerful man in Nevada. In the mid-1970s, he appeared before a grand jury to testify about money he had given to the local sheriff. "That wasn't no bribe," Benny said. "If that there sheriff hadn't paid it back, I'd have made him wash dishes for me in the kitchen." (The sheriff, incidentally, was said to be the second most powerful man in Nevada.) Later, when he was asked why he gave money to political candidates, including Gerald Ford, he replied, "For favors, what else?" The sheriff was indicted on a tax charge and found not guilty.

Tough times may make tough people, but age, reputation, and great wealth turn tough people into lovable old characters. Although the running of the casino is now in the hands of Jack Binion, Benny still holds court every day in the Sombrero Room, the Horseshoe's restaurant, at a table overlooking the casino that is permanently reserved for him and his cronies. He wears a cowboy shirt with solid-gold buttons, eyes the people coming through the door, greets some, and spends a great deal of time on a private telephone that hangs on the wall behind his chair. Last April, he was back in the news following the publication of a book by a Mafia informant who alleged that Benny had once taken out a $200,000 contract with a hit man. "Two hundred grand, never," an indignant friend said. "Two, maybe. In casino credits." Benny himself seemed unperturbed by the allegation.

That, too, was in character. "He doesn't care," said Jack Straus, one of the most formidable of all the poker professionals, and certainly the wittiest. "I get tired of hearing gamblers tell hero stories about themselves — how four big guys jumped them and they whipped the four dudes and seduced all the beautiful women. When Benny tells a story, he's the fool, he's the coward. I finally got to realizing that here is a man who knows exactly where he's at. He isn't the least bit interested in impressing you, because he knows who he really is. And he pays you the compliment of assuming that you know, too."

During the month of the World Series of Poker, Benny also has no time to try to impress anyone. Journalists and photographers flood in to the Horseshoe from all over the world, television teams trail their cables around the poker room, stick the snouts of their cameras over the players' shoulders, and fuss with the lights, while the players arrive from every corner of America and also from London, Paris, Athens, Sydney, Oslo, and Dublin. "In the Old West, they used to have trappers' rendezvous every four years," said Straus. "All the mountain men and people who lived up in the wilderness would get together in a certain spot to swap stories, have wrestling matches and canoe races, and see their friends. This is our trappers' rendezvous, but we have it every year."

The World Series was first held in 1970, but the idea of it originated in 1949, when Nick the Greek Dandalos arrived in Las Vegas looking for a high-stakes poker game. There were plenty of big games in town even then, but all of them were ring games, with seven or eight players, and all were played with limits on the betting. The Greek wanted to play no-limit poker, head-up with a single opponent. Benny Binion, with a shrewd eye for free publicity for his recently acquired casino, offered to set up a game, provided it was played in public. When the Greek agreed, Binion called Johnny Moss, in Dallas.

Moss, who now has the face of an irritable basilisk, was forty-two at the time, smooth-cheeked, thin-haired, with wide-set, hooded eyes and a thin, scrolled mouth. He had been brought up on the streets of Dallas, a newsboy when he was eight, a telegraph messenger at nine. If you ask him when he learned to play cards, he tells you, with relish, that he learned how to cheat before he learned how to play. "Dealin' from the bottom of the pack, deal-in' seconds, usin' mirrors, markin' cards, fadin' the dice — everythin' about cheatin'," he says. "We thought we were smart. Everybody we looked at was a sucker. The suckers had money an' we didn't. I could make a livin', but it warn't a good livin'. I could never get hold of a lot of money, like a sucker could, so in time I come to see it was better to be a sucker. For sixty years now, I've been a sucker. But I'm hard to beat." At the age of fifteen, like a reformed criminal turning state's evidence, he quit cheating and went to work in a gambling house called The Otter's Club in Dallas as a lookout man, to protect the players against cheaters. It was there that he began to play cards seriously, and by the age of nineteen he was a road gambler, playing all over the Southwest, wherever the action was good, often staked by Benny Binion. But it was a precarious existence. "Every time I go into a game, the cheaters are there, the thieves are there, the hijackers are there, the police are after you, the rangers are after you," he says. "Then you have to get in an' beat the cards. You have to win an' get out with the money." For years, he played with a revolver in his jacket pocket at the table and a double-barreled .410 shotgun on the back seat of his car. "I've been arrested five or six times for carryin' that there shotgun," he says. "I tell 'em I'm out bird huntin', an' I pay a two-hunnerd-dollar fine. But I have buckshot in my shells, an' they say, 'You shoot a bird, you blow it all to pieces.' I say, 'This is for a two-legged human bird, not a hummingbird.' On the road, you jus' have to be prepared. If they know you carry a shotgun into your hotel room with you, they better not be there waitin'. Some places are easier to stick up than others." Then he adds, mildly, "Not that I'm mean or nothin'."

Moss played through the East Texas oil boom, and he played through the Depression. He also took up golf, which he played as brilliantly as poker and for equally exorbitant sums of money — sometimes for as much as $100,000 a round, often for $1000 a hole. But he had never been to Las Vegas, and when Benny Binion called him in 1949 he was exhausted from a four-day poker marathon. Nevertheless, he caught the first plane from Dallas, took a cab to the Horseshoe, shook hands with the Greek, and sat down immediately to play.

In the weeks that followed, the Greek got his action and Binion got his publicity, to a degree that neither of them could have imagined. The game lasted for five months, with breaks for sleep every four or five days, although the Greek, who was fifteen years older than Moss, spent most of his nonpoker time at the craps tables and needled Moss about his frailty, saying, "What are you going to do, Johnny — sleep your life away?" But even before the first break the table, which Benny had thoughtfully positioned near the entrance to the casino, was surrounded by crowds six deep, drawn by rumors of the biggest game the town had ever seen.

They began by playing five-card stud — "not my real strong game," Moss says — and during the weeks of this, while occasional players came and went, buying themselves in with a minimum stake of $10,000, Moss and the Greek played what has since become one of the most famous and expensive hands in the history of poker.

Five-card stud is the most classic of the games. Each of the players antes an agreed sum and on the first deal receives two cards — one face down, or in the hole, the other face up. They bet, and are then dealt three more cards face up, one at a time, checking (that is, not betting), betting, or folding after each card. As Moss and the Greek were playing it, each anted $100, and the man with the lowest exposed card "brought it in" — that is, was forced to bet, in this case $200. Before this particular deal started, each had about a quarter of a million dollars' worth of chips in front of him; by the time it was over, the entire half-million dollars was in the pot.

Moss's first two cards were a nine in the hole and a six exposed; the Greek was showing a seven. Moss tells the story now, as he has told it often before, with a kind of chewed-up relish. His Texas drawl is so thick and slurred that it sounds at times like a foreign language, but the sentences are as economical as telegrams: "Low man brings it in. I bet two hunnerd with a six, he raises fifteen hunnerd or two thousand, I call him. The next card comes, I catch a nine, he catches a six. I got two nines then. I make a good bet — five thousand, maybe — an' he plays back at me, twenny-five thousand. I jus' call him. I'm figurin' to take all that money of his, an' I don't wanna scare him none. The next card comes, he catches a trey, I catch a deuce. Ain't nuttin' he got can beat my two nines. I check then to trap him, an' he bets, jus' like I wanted. So I raise him *wa-ay* up there, an' he calls. I got him in there, all right. There's a hunnerd thousand dollars in that pot — maybe more; I don't know exactly — an' I'm a-winnin' it. On the end, I catch a trey, he catches a jack. He's high now with the jack an' he bets fifty thousand. I cain't put him on no jack in the hole, you know. He ain't gonna pay all that money jus' for the chance to outdraw me. I don't care what he catches, he's gotta beat those two nines of mine. So I move in with the rest of my money."

Nick Dandalos was fifty-seven years old, tall, trim, and polite. He had a degree from an English university and was reputed to have broken all the gamblers on the East Coast, including the legendary Arnold Rothstein, winning $60 million in the process. In the moments of silence after Moss pushed what remained of his quarter of a million dollars' worth of chips into the center, the Greek eyed him, upright and unblinking, and then said softly, "Mr. Moss, I think I have a jack in the hole."

"Greek," Moss replied, "if you got a jack down there, you're liable to win yourself one hell of a pot."

There was another aching silence, and then the Greek carefully pushed his own chips forward and turned over his hole card. It was the jack of diamonds.

"He outdrew me," Moss says now. "We had about two hunnerd an' fifty thousand dollars apiece in that pot, and he win it. But that was all right. I broke him anyway."

That is the old man talking, secure in his fame and his investments, as remorseless now as he was then, the kind of character that John Wayne was fond of portraying — true grit without forgiveness, to be admired, but from a safe distance. Even now, only the hardest players are willing to sit down with him. In the course of their marathon, Moss and Nick the Greek played most forms of poker. They switched from five-card stud to draw, seven-card stud, seven-card high-low split, and both forms of lowball — ace-to-the-five and deuce-to-the-seven — and, gradually, Moss wore his opponent down. After almost exactly five months, the Greek lost his last pot, smiled courteously, and said in his soft voice, "Mr. Moss, I have to let you go." He bowed slightly and went upstairs to bed. Precisely how much he had lost is not certain; the rumor says two million.

In 1970, the Binions decided to restage a battle of the giants by inviting the top professionals to play in public. There was no official prize money, and the champion was elected democratically by the assembled players. The man they chose was Johnny Moss. "In those days, it warn't no one game an' it warn't no freeze-out," he says. "You had to win all the games, win all the money. Then you're the best player, an' they vote on you. A lot of gamblers hate me, but they still vote on me being the best player in the world. It was pretty nice, you know, because there were a lot of good players in town. But most good players are only good at one game, an' I was good at 'em all. I win all five games that year an' they give me a big trophy. In '74, they give me this here gold bracelet with the date engraved on the back." The bracelet on his wrist, like his watch strap, is made up of extravagant chunks of gold and looks heavy enough for a Georgia chain gang. "I win a silver cup, too — solid silver, engraved. In all, it must have weighed forty pounds."

Moss is now seventy-five years old, his eyes hooded and bleak, his face like saddle leather, deep lines carved from his nose almost to his chin, his rather elegantly shaped mouth retracted in permanent distaste. But he is still playing most nights and still winning. In 1981, he celebrated his fifty-fifth wedding anniversary by winning the seven-card high-low split event of the World Series against a lowering, impassive amateur with a ramrod back from Orlando, Florida, who looked like central casting's idea of a CIA heavy, although by trade he was an appliance repairman.

The final was as ritualized as a tribal dance. The winner of the third prize was a bundle of nervous tics in a blue satin track suit. He joggled his feet up and down ceaselessly, twitched, jerked, played with his chips, twisted about in his chair — a man with so many of what poker players call "tells" that no one was seemingly significant. But after he was eliminated the table became an island of stillness and concentration in the babble of the casino. Moss and the man from Orlando loomed erect in their chairs, barely moving. Neither of them looked at his seventh card when it was dealt to him, face down. Each shuffled it in with his hole cards, and then they eyed each other steadily for what seemed like minutes on end. At last, they lifted the corners of their hole cards, peered at them blankly, and bet without speaking, in stacks of black and gray chips. As the game went on, Moss, who was wearing a pale brown suit flecked with darker brown, like a chocolate chip cookie, took off his heavy gold bracelet and watch and laid them on the table beside his chips. His shirt was open, showing a necklace of heavy twisted gold. The railbirds eyed all this treasure with delight. They love Moss, and he plays to them in a dead-pan way, his old lizard eyes registering something almost like pleasure whenever they applaud a win. But he mutters angrily when he loses a big pot, and the sense of threat he exudes increases. He is said to be superstitious, and when he was running a poker room on the Strip he once fired a dealer who consistently gave him bad cards. In ominousness, however, he and his baleful opponent from Florida seemed well matched.

The prize money was piled at one corner of the table in packets of crisp hundred-dollar bills: $33,500 for the winner, $13,400 for the runner-up. One of Binion's giant security guards sat beside it, a Roman gladiator in desert brown, eyes fixed grimly on the cash — the only person there not watching the players or the cards.

It took Moss perhaps two hours head-to-head to clean out his opponent. Afterward, he and his wife, Virgie, helped the Binions and other gambling friends devour a bilious anniversary cake in the Sombrero Room. That night, Moss was playing again.

Since that first meeting at Binion's, in 1970, when the top professionals elected Moss champion, the tourna-ment has expanded and the rules have changed. The contestants now buy themselves into each event — the stakes vary from $400 for the women's seven-card stud to $10,000 for the main events — and play freeze-out; that is, they play until they have no more chips in front of them, and one man has won them all. In 1971, Moss won the main title outright from six fellow professionals; he was beaten in the final by Puggy Pearson in 1973; and he won it again the following year, at the age of sixty-seven. By 1981, there were twelve separate competitions, and the number of contestants for the world title had risen to seventy-five, the $750,000 prize money being divided on a sliding scale among the nine players who reached the final table, the winner taking half, the runner-up 20 percent, and so on down to 2 percent each for the seventh, eighth, and ninth placed.

Nearly all forms of poker are played during the tournament except five-card stud, which now seems too slow-paced and inflexible to interest the top players. But the game that decides who shall win the title of World Champion is hold 'em, which originated in Texas toward the end of the last century and is still regarded with suspicion outside the Southwest. (I myself have tried, and failed, to introduce it into two regular New York poker games. In London, oddly, poker players are less inflexible.) Hold 'em is a variation of seven-card stud with communal exposed cards. Each player antes and is dealt two cards face down; the man to the left of the dealer is forced to bet. (In casinos, where there is a professional, nonplaying dealer, an object like a small hockey puck, called the button, is placed in front of each player in turn to indicate that he is "dealer" for that hand.) The other players either see the bet, raise it, or fold. Then three communal cards, called the flop, are dealt face up in the center of the table, and there is another round of betting, but this time the players may check. Then two more cards — known as Fourth Street and Fifth Street — are dealt face up, one at a time, with a round of betting after each. The five cards in the center are common to all the players, who use them in combination with their hole cards to make the strongest possible hands.

The variations and subtleties are infinite. A pair of aces in the hole is the strongest start, but after the flop anything is possible: a small pair in the hole suddenly becomes three of a kind (called a "set" in Vegas); two connecting or suited cards turn into a straight or a flush. The complexities are so great that Doyle Brunson, in his treatise on advanced poker, devotes two hundred pages to hold 'em — three or four times the space allowed for any other form of poker. "Hold 'em is to stud and draw what chess is to checkers," Johnny Moss has said. It is a game of wits and psychology and position, of bluffing, thrust, and counterthrust, and depends more on skill and character than on receiving good cards. Like Kenny Rogers's gambler, "You've got to know when to hold 'em, Know when to fold 'em, Know when to walk away, And know when to run."

Hold 'em is played in a number of Las Vegas casinos, but nearly always with a limit on the bet allowed. Even the Golden Nugget — the frontier-style casino right across the street from the Horseshoe — though it boasts the largest, busiest poker room in town and specializes in hold 'em, rarely has games with a limit higher than $30 on the first two rounds of betting and $60 on Fourth and Fifth Street, with a maximum of four raises a round. In what is called a jammed pot, where two or more players have very strong cards and are reraising each other as much as possible, that is enough to lose several hundred dollars a hand, yet this is small beer to the top professionals, most of whom look down on limit poker as an unimaginative, mechanical game. Jack Straus described it contemptuously as "a disciplined job," saying, "Anybody who wants to work out the mathematics can be a limit player and chisel out an existence. You just have to condition yourself to sit there and wait." Serious players, he meant, know the odds on filling a straight or a flush or a full house with one or two cards to come. In limit poker, where they also know precisely how much this will cost them and how much money the pot will be offering if they call or raise or are reraised, every move can be reduced to mathematics and probabilities. The difference between the top limit players and those who are slightly less good is in the ability to get the maximum from winning hands and lose the minimum when the hands are weak.

When the champions play limit poker, they play with limits so high that the antes alone will destroy the conservative player while he waits. Moss told me of one seven-card stud game in which the ante was $800, the dealer bet $1600 blind (without looking at the cards he had been dealt), the low card brought it in for $3200, and the opening raise was to $6400. "I won eight hundred and seventy thousand dollars that night — the most I ever did make in one game," he said. "The biggest check" — chip — "they had was a hunnerd-dollar black. I had racks of 'em piled up on the floor beside my chair; there warn't no room on the table." I asked him who had been playing. "Coast gamblers, guys from Los Angeles," he answered, and added helpfully, "Rich people, mostly." "I suspect," a mutual friend told me, "that not too much tax had been paid on that money. It wasn't a poker game; it was a Laundromat."

There are few limit games as awesome as that, although seven-card stud, with its five betting intervals, is always played with limits in Vegas, often $300 and $600, sometimes $500 and $1000, occasionally higher. At those dizzy altitudes, the same skill and imagination are required as in no-limit poker. The cheaper the games, the more like hard work they become. For twenty-four of the twenty-seven nights I was in Vegas, I played three-dollar- and six-dollar-limit hold 'em at the Golden Nugget: eleven players to a table, of whom eight were usually locals — retired truck drivers and farmers, unretired divorcées eking out their alimony, and always two or three dealers from the higher-limit games using their rest periods to test their skills. We would sit there, all of us, throwing away hand after hand after hand, waiting for ironclad certainties — "the nuts" — or an edge, or, better still, for a weary tourist to drive in off the desert and start chasing his luck. It was an exercise in discipline and patience, and had less in common with gambling than with a term in the salt mines.

Across the road at Binion's, however, hold 'em is played without limit. This means that after the obligatory opening bets a player may move in with all the chips he has in front of him, no matter how much is in the pot. When Amarillo Slim Preston won the title from Puggy Pearson, in 1972, for example, he bet his whole stack — $51,000 — into a pot containing a mere $2000. "It feels better in," he announced to the goggling railbirds. Puggy decided he was bluffing, called, and lost.

The opportunities for bluffing are as infinite as the

psychological nuances. (Amarillo Slim had previously set Puggy up by raising blind every bet Puggy made, and so stealing pots with worthless cards. But when he made his big move he had a strong hand and Puggy was ready to call.) "No-limit is a test of intestinal fortitude," Jack Straus has said. Like the other top players, he judges his opponents not by their mathematical ability but by what they call "heart" — the courage to bet *all* their money when they reckon that the odds are in their favor. Crandall Addington, a supremely elegant Texan, who regularly sets the sartorial standard for the tournament, and who, unlike the other members of the poker elite, plays more for pleasure than for money, since he has already made his millions in real estate and oil, has said, "Limit poker is a science, but no-limit is an art. In limit, you are shooting at a target. In no-limit, the target comes alive and shoots back at you."

An example is one of the heaviest of the perpetual side games, when Addington, Straus, Brunson, and Puggy Pearson were wisecracking, needling, and outsmarting each other from behind mountains of chips. Also at the table was Jesse Alto, a car dealer from Houston and a regular contender in the World Series, who placed second in 1976 and fifth in 1978. Alto is about fifty years old, trim, compact, with graying hair and heavy forearms, on one of them a small tattoo slightly smeared, as if he had tried to erase it. It contrasts oddly with his platinum Audemars-Piguet watch. He is a complex man with a complex background: his parents were Lebanese, but he was born in Mexico and raised in Israel; he arrived in Texas as a deckhand on a cargo ship when he was nineteen, and has lived there ever since. Many of the top poker players are ex-athletes — both Brunson and Straus were basketball stars at school — but Alto is one of the few who have remained more or less permanently in training, through racquetball and golf. In a world of marathon players, he has a reputation for exceptional stamina; he once played for a whole week without losing his concentration. He is also a gifted linguist.

Before the flop, Alto raised the opening bet, then called when he was modestly reraised by Straus. The other players folded. The flop came king, ten, eight, of different suits. Alto, who had a king and eight of diamonds in the hole, checked in order to trap Straus. Straus paused, then bet $1000 — again, modestly by the standards of the game, but large enough for a bluff. This was what Alto had been hoping for; with his two pairs, kings and eights, he raised $5000.

Straus slumped even further in his chair. He is over six and a half feet tall — his nickname is Treetops — but sits hunched at the table, shoulders forward, curly gray hair and curly gray beard sunk between them, as though denying his size. Away from the poker table as well as at it, he is a hunter — a crack shot — and he has a marksman's eyes: dark blue, slanting down from right to left, the left eye always slightly closed, like a man taking aim. He watched Alto in silence for a long time, but Alto did not stir. Then he cupped his hands around his cards and squeezed them slightly upward with his thumbs. Another pause. Then quickly, almost fretfully, he pushed several stacks of chips into the center.

The dealer counted them carefully and said, "Raise thirty thousand dollars."

The target had come alive and was shooting back.

Alto did not move, but his erect back seemed to curve infinitesimally, as if under the pressure of a great weight.

He sat considering the alternatives while Puggy Pearson lit a giant cigar. Did Straus have a king and an ace in the hole, or even two pairs, like Alto himself? Or did he have a pair that gave him, with the flop, a set of kings or tens or eights? Or did he have a queen and a jack in the hole and so he was betting "on the come," hoping to complete a straight? Or, since this was Jack Straus, the master of the withering bluff and a man with a reputation for total fearlessness — he once bet $100,000 on the outcome of a high-school basketball game — was he simply bluffing?

For long, empty minutes, the two players faced each other across the table, unmoving and unspeaking, like figures in stone. Finally, Alto counted out his chips and pushed them gloomily forward. Straus's bet had set him in for all his money, so there would be no more betting. He turned over his king and eight. Straus nodded, and then, in a matter-of-fact way, turned over his hole cards: two tens. The ten in the center had given him a set of three, and only another king could save Alto. The dealer burned — discarded — the top card and dealt a seven, burned the next card and dealt a four. The three tens were good.

In hold 'em at this level, the target does not just shoot back, it also shifts about like a will-o'-the-wisp, maneuvering for position. In the previous hour, Straus had twice bet in precisely the same pattern, but with far weaker cards; both times, Alto had called him and won. The only difference was that the sums involved had been much smaller — a few thousand rather than tens of thousands. I had watched those two earlier hands uncomprehending, for it seemed — even to an outsider and a relative novice like me — that Straus was betting on losing cards. Yet I was also aware that if I knew it so did he, since one of the many gifts that separate the professionals from the amateurs is the ability to read their opponents' hands with uncanny accuracy from the tiniest clues: timing, position, the way their fingers move their chips, even the pulse beat in their neck. In *Super/System*, Doyle Brunson gives numerous instances of how and why he knew precisely which cards his opponent had in the hole. Just two days before that side game between Straus and Alto, Stuart Ungar, who won the World Championship in 1980, at the age of twenty-six, had called a last bet of several hundred dollars in a game of seven-card stud holding only a pair of threes, then raked in the pot contemptuously before his opponent showed his down cards, knowing without a flicker of doubt that all the other man had in the hole "was dreams." Straus, although in 1981 he still had not yet won the championship, has the same unnerving clairvoyance. Like all the top professionals, he has played for so long and with such concentration that nothing is new or unfamiliar or unfathomable. Yet there he was, apparently throwing away money as carelessly as any tyro. I was wrong, of course. Straus had been setting Alto up for the kill, raising his confidence, lulling him into the belief that he, Straus, was playing loosely, so that when his moment came he could make the same ploy with a monster hand and Alto would call him. The two losing hands were investments that finally yielded a disproportionate return — $8000 to make $40,000.

3

—T this level, gambling is a business," Jack Binion told me one day. "These guys are trying to beat each other in the subtlest possible ways, but if they wanted to rationalize it they could say it is a high-risk, high-return investment that is also fun to do." In business terms, the ten-minute transaction between Straus and Alto was nothing very remarkable. It was equally unremarkable in terms of the games played all day and every day when the poker room at the Horseshoe is open. Yet it produced for the winner enough money to support an average family for a year in comfort.

Granted, average wage earners do not play high-stakes poker in Las Vegas. There are estimated to be over fifty-six million poker players in the United States alone, and only two or three hundred of them ever graduate to the games at Binion's; of those players, perhaps twenty would stand a chance in the really big games. Even so, the casualness and imperturbability with which that elite handles huge sums of money is beyond ordinary understanding. It is a question not just of a different level of skill but of a different ordering of reality.

Not long before Straus won his big pot from Alto, he had removed his cash from the table when the players broke for lunch, leaving at his place about $15,000 worth of chips. When the game resumed, Brunson gestured toward Straus's stack and said, "Playing cheap today, Jack?" Straus looked down at the towers of black chips in front of him and feigned sheepishness. "I plumb forgot I didn't have any money out there," he said. "No wonder I felt naked." And he pulled from his trouser pockets seven or eight banded packets of $5000 each and dumped them carelessly on the table.

"The sums involved are beyond reason. They blow your mind." That was said to me not by an outsider but by A. J. Myers, a regular and successful player, who in 1981 won the biggest of the seven-card stud competitions, walking away with $67,500 prize money. Myers, a retired real estate broker who looks like a fleshy West Coast version of Saul Bellow — professorial half-glasses perched on the end of his nose, red floral band around his straw hat — plays regularly in the big seven-stud games with the top professionals, owns a condominium in town, and commutes from his home in Beverly Hills, sometimes as often as a dozen times a year. Yet he still finds it hard to adjust to the professional gamblers' indifference to money. "They look at me, and there is absolutely no understanding be-

tween us," he told me. "They will bet on a ball game —
football, basketball, baseball — sums that stagger the
imagination. I know many wealthy people, some of them
worth well over a hundred million, who would never bet
more than a couple of hundred dollars on a game, because
they would feel terrible if they lost. Yet some of the gamblers here, who are worth nothing compared with those
people, will bet a hundred thousand without blinking. Most
of them are average golfers — they shoot in the middle
eighties — but at the end of a match they regularly settle
up for fifty or a hundred thousand dollars. Even the golf
pros don't play for that kind of money, and if they did
they probably wouldn't be able to hold a putter. If a golf
pro who shot seventy played a gambler who shot eighty-
two and gave him the right handicap, he would lose all
the time. The pressure would be too much for him; for
the gambler, it is a stimulus."

"Right," said Straus. "I even drive farther when the
stakes are high."

In poker, as in golf, at least they are betting on their
own skills. The cards go round, but in the end the best
players win. When the poker players bet on sports, however, they are putting down gigantic sums on events
wholly beyond their control. Even the late Arnold Rothstein managed to fix the baseball World Series only once.
"Players who make tremendous amounts of money
through their talents at the poker table go out and destroy
it betting on things they have no control over," Myers said.

We were sitting in the Sombrero Room with Myers's
wife and his daughter, a California Matisse odalisque who
had recently returned from a grand tour of Europe. They
nodded understandingly, knowing that Myers had earned
his right to disapprove by surviving a gambling fever as

virulent as any junkie's addiction. He first came to Las Vegas to shoot craps. He had a princely credit line at all the major hotels and was "comped" — provided with a free luxury suite, free food and drink, and whatever other indulgence he fancied ("all the fringe benefits of being a big sucker," he called it) — wherever he went. He had run through a fortune "in taxed money" before he realized that his dream life in Vegas was endangering his real life at home.

"So I stopped."

"Just like that?"

"I believe in will power. And in responsibility to my family. If I'd been alone, perhaps I wouldn't have quit. But with a wife and child I had to take stock of myself. I knew there was nothing in the world could support the habit I had."

"Then what?"

"I learned to play blackjack, which afforded me the luxury of sitting down while I gambled rather than standing at a craps table and wearing myself out. In very short order, I was an expert, and the casinos wouldn't allow me to play."

So he turned to poker, which he had played for years in relatively small-stakes games in California. "At first, I was very much in awe of the professionals and consequently found it hard to compete," he told me. "I'm not really talking about the level of their skill, I'm talking about money. The games were of a size I wasn't used to, and until you get used to the high stakes you pull in your horns and play too conservatively. The money freezes you up, and you become tight-weak. You try not to play until you have an unbeatable hand, and when someone makes a big bet at you you automatically assume the worst. The tight-weak player is the kind the pros most love to play with; they run rings around him. But in time I got used to the size of the game. It is a question of respect, not fear. I'm a wealthy guy, and I don't believe I was ever really afraid of the big money. But it took me a while to realize that if I had too much respect for the money I couldn't play properly. Chips are like a bag of beans; they have a relative value and are worthless until the game is over. That is the only attitude you can have in high-stakes poker.

"Even so, I still prefer a medium-sized game, like the two-hundred-dollar-and-four-hundred-dollar limit, where if you're going bad you can lose twenty or thirty thousand dollars. The highest I've played is five-hundred-and-thousand, where you can easily lose a hundred thousand dollars. They've begged me to play in the thousand-and-two-thousand-dollar game, but I have always refused. It was just too high; I didn't want it to affect my game. And the truth is, I don't even like the five-hundred-and-thousand-dollar limit. There is too much money involved. It offends my sensibilities. Yet time and again I've been in medium-sized games with players who don't look as if they could afford to play fifteen-and-thirty-dollar limit, and they have pleaded with me to raise the stakes. God knows where the money comes from, yet if they lose they always pay.

"It offends my sensibilities." His wife nodded, the odalisque daughter smiled, and Myers's eerie resemblance to Saul Bellow increased. His judgment seemed, in the circumstances, the right and proper one. Yet in the noisy gloom of Binion's, with the midday heat blasting the street outside and the signs blazing and jumping like a fever, the words he used were as foreign as Urdu — like the exhibition of pictures painted by local schoolchildren that lined the corridors of McCarran Airport when I arrived. KIDS LIVE IN VEGAS, TOO, the signs repeated, but the only kids I saw were the stunned waifs half asleep on the carpeted sidewalk outside the Golden Nugget, waiting for their parents to blow the week's housekeeping, and the lost souls, faces sticky with cotton candy, wandering around the sideshows on the mezzanine of Circus-Circus. Las Vegas is no more a place for childhood than it is a place for sensibility. It is a town without grace and without nuance, where the only useful virtues are experience, survival, and money.

"In Vegas, they weigh you up in gold," said Straus. "They call it the golden rule: the man who has the gold makes the rules." They also say that it is the only town where visitors are made to think that a hundred-dollar bill will not buy a loaf of bread. Ulvis Alberts, for example, is a freelance photographer who has covered the poker tournament for the last five years and whose marvelously atmospheric portraits of the players were published in 1981 in a collection called *Poker Face*. During his first visit to Binion's, a number of the contestants asked to buy blowups of the pictures he had taken of them. "That will be seventy-five dollars," he said, and suddenly there was a problem: when the gamblers pulled out their giant wads of cash none of them had change. "So I charged a hundred dollars," he told me, "and everyone was happy."

Another example: Chip Reese has been in Las Vegas since 1974. His hair is blond and unruly, his plumpness is turning to fat, and his round face appears jolly until you see his eyes. He dresses in extravagantly colored velvet track suits, but this Vegas deshabille is misleading:

his background is solid upper-middle-class Ohio, and he graduated from Dartmouth. At Dartmouth, however, the pattern was already set; after he left, the Big Daddy Lipinski Poker Room at the Beta Theta Pi house was renamed the David E. Reese Memorial Card Room, and a plaque was put up in his honor, listing the names of the fraternity brothers he had fleeced during his four years' residence. To raise money for law school, he took a job as a manufacturer's representative, but he hated it, despite the pay, and quit after nine months. On his way out to see a friend in California, he stopped off in Vegas for a weekend. He had $400 in his pocket when he sat down in a $20-limit seven-card stud game; at the end of the first day, he had won $800; the next day he won $1000; within a fortnight he was $25,000 ahead. He has been in Vegas ever since, and now runs the poker room at the Dunes. Reese is rumored to have won a couple of million dollars in his first three years in town. This may or may not be true. What is certain is that the continual movement of huge sums of money across the poker table has fractured his sense of reality. "I'd like to be able to say I'm in tune with world affairs and worried about my budget," he told me. His years in Nevada have not affected his accent; his voice is crisp and Ivy League, without a trace of drawl. "But when I play poker for hundreds of thousands of dollars a day what do I care if a Popsicle costs ten cents here and twelve cents there? Big-limit poker is a separate world, and makes it hard to relate to other aspects of what's going on. Hundred-dollar bills in Vegas are like one-dollar bills anywhere else. I don't even carry dollar bills except to tip the cocktail waitresses, and I can't remember the last time I had coins in my pockets. In other towns, these habits can cause a prob-

41

lem: I've stopped at a drive-in for a hamburger, and when the bill came for five dollars I've pulled out a hundred-dollar bill. They look at me as if I were some kind of thief, and say, 'We can't change this.' You don't think about these things until they happen to you."

The degree to which Reese fails to think about these things is famous around town. He is rumored to have lost in his own house every piece of jewelry he has ever owned, and for a period to have paid without question a monthly water bill of two thousand dollars. After some time, the water company discovered that the pipe supplying his house had broken and was flooding the area for acres around. Reese himself had not noticed.

"Money means nothing," he told me. "If you really cared about it, you wouldn't be able to sit down at a poker table and bluff off fifty thousand dollars. If I thought what that could buy me, I could not be a good player. Money is just the yardstick by which you measure your success. In Monopoly, you try to win all the cash by the end of the game. It's the same in poker: you treat chips like play money and don't think about it until it's all over."

It is this money element that makes poker different from all other card games. According to Terence Reese, who has captained the English bridge team, there is little to choose between bridge and poker in terms of skill. Yet poker looks like a gambling game — and for years was classified as such by the British Gaming Board — because, unlike bridge, it must be played for money. Chips are not just a way of keeping score; they combine with the cards to form the very language of the game. What you do with your chips — how and when you bet or check or raise — is a way of communicating with your opponents. "You ask subtle questions with your chips," said the subtle Crandall Addington. The questions you ask and the answers you receive may be misleading — a gigantic bet may be a sign of weakness, an attempt to drive the other players out of the pot because you do not have the hand you purport to have — but the combination of cards and money and position at the table creates a complex pattern of information (or illusion) that controls the flow of the game. In poker, betting and what is called "money management" are as much an art as reading the cards and judging the probabilities.

"In order to play high-stakes poker, you need to have a total disregard for money," Doyle Brunson said. "It is just an instrument, and the only time you notice it is when you run out." Among the top players, however, running out of money is a relative concept. Although they all announce, with pride, that every real pro has gone broke more times than he can count, being out of money does not seem to affect their spendthrift habits. Johnny Moss told me that when he was younger he had had no difficulty in borrowing $10,000 to play poker but had known no one he could ask for $500 simply to get out of town. He also said that gamblers drove the best cars, wore the best clothes, stayed at the best hotels, got the best-looking women, and lived like millionaires even when they were broke; the amount of money they had at any particular moment did not alter their habits one jot.

Not long ago, for example, Stu Ungar, the 1980 World Champion, who, like Chip Reese, is rumored to have turned over millions of dollars in a couple of years in Las Vegas, winning at cards, losing at sports betting, was due to play a game in Reno. But he missed the plane at McCarran, and the next departure was four hours later. Without hesitating, he hired a private jet. The commercial flight would have cost him $30, and the charter cost him $1200, but his destination was a high-stakes game, so there seemed no point in hanging around.

"I'd go to the moon if they were anteing high enough," said Bobby Baldwin, another young World Championship winner. Meanwhile, he commutes the 1180 miles to Las Vegas from his home, in Tulsa, and reckons to spend $20,000 a year on air fares. "One night, I chartered a Lear jet and then found the game had broken up while I was airborne," he told me. He shrugged laconically. "Dry run." As for his living expenses, he said, "I have to make fifteen to twenty thousand dollars a month to break even. To tell you the truth, my wife and I never go near a supermarket. Our groceries are delivered to our home and put in the kitchen cabinets by the delivery boy." Baldwin is not given to boasting; he has a student's small, bespectacled face under a halo of curls, and his manner — away from the poker table — is preternaturally modest. He was merely indicating the degree to which high-stakes poker inoculates the players against economic reality. Money is no longer money to the professionals; it is like a wrench to a plumber — a tool of the trade. It is also, most often, not a green treasury bill validated by a president's face but a colored plastic disc stamped with a number and the name of a casino. A New York gambler who goes by the name of Big Julie once remarked sagely, "The guy who invented gambling was bright, but the guy who invented the chip was a genius." The chip is like a conjurer's sleight of hand that turns an egg into a billiard ball, a necessity of life into a plaything, reality into illusion. Players who freeze up at the sight of a fifty-dollar bill, thinking it could buy them a week's food at the super-

44

market, will toss two green chips into the pot without even hesitating if the odds are right. "Chips don't have a home," said Jack Straus. "People will play much higher with chips than they will with cash. For some reason, it is hard for inferior players to turn loose of money, but give them chips and they get caught up, mesmerized by the game."

Chips, in fact, are the currency of Las Vegas. When a gambler arranges a line of credit with a casino, he takes the money in chips. You tip with them, pay for meals and drink and sex with them, and could probably buy goods with them in the stores. The better adjusted to them you become, the further reality recedes. To hand over a couple of pieces of unimposing black plastic and receive for them a two-hundred-dollar jacket is no longer a business transaction, it is magic. "This town hypnotizes people," Doyle Brunson said. "Guys who won't bet twenty dollars at home come out here and bet five hundred or a thousand without even thinking — particularly during the poker tournament. Playing constantly for a month or more is like being in a pressure cooker. If you are not careful, you reach boiling point and explode. Then you just throw your money away. They keep hammering and hammering at you, until you lose touch with reality about everything. That's when people go off and lose huge sums."

Early one evening, I shared a table in the Sombrero Room with a young cowboy from east Texas. His white T-shirt was soiled, his jeans were frayed, and a downy, struggling mustache made him look even younger than he was, which was twenty-four. Between mouthfuls of fried chicken, he explained to me in great detail the

45

hands on which he had been outdrawn that day. He had lost $25,000 in eight hours, but did not seem particularly concerned.

A couple of days later, Eric Drache wandered into the Sombrero Room, the social hub of the tournament, looking as cheerful as always but vaguely preoccupied. Drache, who is one of the world's best seven-card stud players, is from New Jersey. He went to Rutgers on a chemistry scholarship but dropped out after two years (he was at the race track on the day of a vital examination), learned to play poker seriously while serving as an MP in Vietnam, ran his own game in New York and New Jersey, came out to Vegas for a weekend with $600, and has never returned East. He won $70,000 in his first three months in town, lost $750,000 in the next two years, won it back, lost, won, and has been on the round-about ever since. He now organizes the World Series for the Binions. He is a witty, highly articulate man with a beautiful English wife — a doctor's daughter from Taunton, Devon, who is studying at Columbia and also plays a mean game of seven-card stud — and apparently limitless reserves of charm and affability.

"How goes it?" I asked.

He shook his head. "Terrible."

"How terrible?"

"One-sixty. I hit a bad streak and threw off ten thousand an hour." He shrugged, laughed, and moved off through the crowded restaurant, chatting and joking with the other players. Twenty minutes later, he returned and paused by my table near the entrance, deep in discussion with another professional. I heard him say, "He owes me ten and a half, plus one-eight from Reno . . ." Then he noticed me still sitting there. "Excuse me," he said. "I didn't see you. Money tends to close your mind to common civility, and I'm negotiating a loan. The worst thing is to play poker with your own money." He and the other man both laughed, then drifted off to the poker tables outside.

That insouciance is the test of the true professionals, but they do not necessarily acquire it from a psychopathic deformation of character, or even from the strong inoculation against the value of money that every visitor receives, willy-nilly, from Las Vegas. It comes, instead, from painful experience. "We used to bet all we had, day after day," said Doyle Brunson. "And every other day we went broke." Out of that emerges a kind of bedrock endurance that manifests itself as an attitude toward money.

"Playing poker for a living gives you backbone," Bobby Baldwin said. "You cannot survive without that intangible quality we call heart. I don't care how bad you are going or how good, you have to stand solid. Poker is a character builder — especially the bad times. The mark of a top player is not how much he wins when he is winning but how he handles his losses. If you win for thirty days in a row, that makes no difference if on the thirty-first you have a bad night, go crazy, and throw it all away. You can't survive that way. In this business, you have to be able to live with adversity. You will have losing nights — a lot of them. You'll go off on some big numbers sometimes. I've lost several hundred thousand in one evening, but I didn't go up to my room and shoot myself; instead, I went to bed and slept like a baby. When some of the guys take a big loss, they sleep like a baby in a different way: they sleep an hour and cry an hour, sleep an hour and cry an hour. But I myself find it easier to sleep when

I lose than when I win. That may sound odd, but it's true. I think the reason is that when I have an extremely bad night I go to bed and escape from it in sleep. But when I've won I'm all pumped up and excited; I can't unwind as quickly as I can when I'm down and semidepressed."

It sounds like a natural and rather graceful code of behavior until you register how much money this quiet, mild-mannered young man from Tulsa is referring to when he talks about "going off on some big numbers" — losses that leave him only "semidepressed." In money matters, the top professionals cultivate toward their own finances a positively corporate, penthouse-suite detachment. Sums that would annihilate an ordinary private citizen seem to them mere hiccups in their annual cash flow.

As usual, it was Straus who put this matter in a human perspective. "If money is your god, you can forget no-limit poker, because it's going to hurt you too much to turn loose of it," he said. "The way I feel about those pieces of green paper is, you can't take them with you and they may not have much value in five years' time, but right now I can take them and trade them in for pleasure, or to bring pleasure to other people. If they had wanted you to hold on to money, they'd have made it with handles on."

People like Straus gravitate to Las Vegas because it is the one place where that total disregard for money essential to the high roller precisely matches the fever that the town induces in everyone. At one end are Straus, Brunson, Baldwin, Drache, Ungar; at the other, the little old ladies with their Dixie cups of change in one hand and an Iron Boy work glove on the other, priming the slots hour after hour, waiting for the shower of jackpot gold that will transform their shabby lives: deus ex machina.

To the poker professionals, the god appeared a couple of years ago in an odd disguise. Jimmy Chagra was a cocaine dealer who is now serving thirty years in the federal penitentiary at Leavenworth for his "continuing criminal enterprise." He came to town for a final fling while he waited for his case to come up before a judge known in Texas as Maximum John. (The day the trial was to begin, the judge, John H. Wood, was shot dead, and Chagra was duly indicted for that, too, but acquitted.) Chagra was to Vegas what the Arab princes are to the London casinos: a Platonic ideal incarnate, a high roller with no tomorrow, backed by the virtually unlimited and untaxed resources of the narcotics business.

In the town's early days, before the operators realized that they could make more profits by scrupulous honesty than they could decently cope with, the casinos were rumored to have been used by the mob for laundering dirty money. Chagra's money was as black as pitch, but he was not interested in cleaning it up — only in enjoying it while he had time. Naturally, the only casino willing to allow him to gamble for the deranged sums he insisted on was Binion's Horseshoe. He played there every night — craps, blackjack, roulette — and during the day he took a little fresh air out on the Dunes golf course with the boys, sometimes for half a million a round. Since he was a good gin rummy player and Binion's poker room was open for the World Series, he decided to learn hold 'em and deuce-to-the-seven Kansas City lowball.

The professionals were delighted to teach him, but even they were awed by the size of the games he wanted to play. The minimum table stake was $50,000, but few of them risked sitting down with so little, because time after time Chagra would throw in $20,000 bets blind, which he said were "just to liven the game up a little." Once the action was properly under way, there would be an average of $2 million on the table every night — "so many checks," said Jack Binion, "that you couldn't see the green baize." Jack Binion does not impress easily, but even now he speaks of Chagra's gambling in puzzled, hushed tones, as he might speak of some inexplicable natural phenomenon. With reason: in the weeks Chagra was there, it is said, he beat the Horseshoe for between $2 million and $3 million at craps and blackjack. Early one morning, he got up from a bad session at poker, strolled across to the craps table, bet $100,000 on a single throw of the dice, won, and went to bed.

Chagra's legend goes right down through the casino hierarchy: during one particularly stormy poker game, he tipped a cocktail waitress $10,000 — two packets of fifty hundred-dollar bills — when she brought him a complimentary bottle of Mountain Valley water.

"In poker, money is power," said Alvin Thomas, alias Titanic Thompson, alias Damon Runyon's Sky Masterson, an old-time road gambler, now deceased, who would bet untold amounts on anything if he thought he had a sufficient edge. But money is power only in the hands of an expert. An innocent journalist once asked Amarillo Slim why a Texas oil millionaire who could not be scared out of a pot would not eventually see off the professionals. "Son," replied Slim, who has a reputation for vivid, folksy imagery, "that millionaire would have as much chance in a game with us as you would of getting a French kiss out of the Statue of Liberty." Likewise Jimmy Chagra: the two or three million he won at craps and blackjack he lost back remorselessly and with interest at the poker table. And the crazed action he inspired brought in another high roller, a local named Major Riddle (Major was his first name, not his rank), who owned the Silverbird and a hefty share of several other Las Vegas casinos. Riddle was in his early seventies when Chagra appeared, but chose to ignore this fact. At one point, he played against Chagra for three days and three nights without a break, until he was called out to a board meeting at the Dunes, of which he was president. He left only on the condition that the game not break up while he was away. "Naturally, you want to beat the guy," said Eric Drache. "But you don't want to kill him." As it happened, Riddle died a few months later, having happily dropped $3 million while Chagra was in town.

When I asked who won all the money, I was given a neutral, poker player's answer: "The cash got distributed pretty good." Only Straus was more forthcoming. He told me, "It was like that TV program *Fantasy Island.* I kept waiting for Tattoo to come on and say it was all a dream: 'Look boss! The plane! The plane!'"

For one gambler, though, the bonanza did not end when Chagra went to the penitentiary. This man had a friend named Travis, who "had got into a little trouble" and was paying for it with six years in Leavenworth. But Travis was also a gambler — his specialty, like Chagra's, was gin rummy — and he owed the man in Las Vegas a favor for the times he had staked Travis when Travis was short of cash. Discreet arrangements were made for Travis to play gin rummy with Chagra on behalf of his friend for a percentage of the profits, all financial transactions to take place outside the penitentiary, between Chagra's connections and the man in Las Vegas. "While everyone was reminiscing about the good old days when Jimmy was in town, I was actually playing him," this man said. "A few weeks later, Travis called me collect from the pen. He said, 'The guy's a pushover. We won fifty-six thousand. Let's go on up. Let's go on up to five hundred grand.' I said, 'Sure, Travis, sure we'll go on up. But slowly does it. Take it easy.' So the connections came through with the money. I paid Travis's percentage into a bank and waited for him to call me collect about the next game. And waited and waited. Weeks went by, then months, and still no word. I thought, That damn fool is playing him with his own money; he'll choke up when Chagra raises it up real high, and get himself wiped out. The next thing I heard, Travis had died of a heart attack. I guess he was so happy with all that money he'd won he just couldn't contain himself. So that was the end of the game. Hard for Travis; hard for me, too."

As is true of all gambling stories, the point of this one is not the score itself but the imaginative coup of scoring in impossible circumstances. According to Mickey Appleman, it is this element of imagination that separates the true high rollers from those who merely grind out a living from cards. Appleman is the odd man out at the tournament — a New York intellectual among the cowboys, clever eyes peering out from under a Harpo Marx mop of blond curls, clothes like a hippie's unmade bed. He grew up on Long Island and emerged from graduate school at Ohio State and Case Western Reserve with a string of qualifications that he is reluctant to mention in the hearing of the other poker players: a master's in education, a master's in statistics, a master's in business administration. "I was supposed to go into the business world, but I didn't want to get a short haircut and wing-tipped shoes," he told me. So he took up community work: in Washington, D.C., after the riots of 1967; at a treatment center for alcoholics in Harlem. He also spent years in assorted styles of psychoanalysis, but when I asked him if analysis had helped his addiction to gambling he answered sharply, "Gambling was never an addiction. On the contrary, it helped me more than analysis. I suffered from depression — I was so entwined with my inner world I never had a chance to enjoy myself. For me, activity was the answer. I took up gambling *after* I finished with psychoanalysis, and the depressions never returned."

But the habit of introspection dies hard, and Appleman has thought about gambling as intently as he has thought about more orthodox subjects. Indeed, introspection and the openness to experience that goes with it are, he thinks, the qualities that distinguish the great players from the pedestrians. "There are no soft spots out here," he said. "They are all good players, with sophisticated techniques that you have to analyze and incorporate into your own play. It's like any other field: you have to develop yourself *and* your game. Poker is a skill, it's an art, it's a science. You have to improve continually and know your own weaknesses. To be successful, you must be realistic. Up to a certain point, you have to believe you're a really good player, but you also have to realize what you're up against. There can be no self-deception. But confidence is a double-edged sword. It's the down side of a gambler that ruins him, not his up side. When you're playing well, you can be as good as anybody, but how you handle yourself under pressure when you're playing badly is the character test that separates the men from the boys. Yet the strange thing is, to be a high roller necessarily means having a down side. Certain individuals come here just to make money; they grind, grind, grind in the small-stakes games, they make a living, and they have no down side. But they have no gamble in them, either, so they will never know the enjoyment of the high roller, the romance of gambling. Poker playing is strictly a business to these small-stakes players, but to the high rollers it's business and it's also pleasure; it's fun, it's a game, it's gamesmanship. After all, what are we all here for at the Horseshoe? When you are playing for hundreds of thousands of dollars, it's not the money. I mean, how much do you need? It's the gamesmanship, the competition, the thrill of letting it all hang out. Poker for big money is a high-risk sport, like driving a racing car. I've always appreciated the high rollers, because pettiness has no part in their lives. The technicians who do well in the small games will never derive the same thrill from it as somebody who is willing to roll it out there. Of course, different types of people look for different levels of satisfaction. I'm a romantic, and for me gambling is a romance. That's what I enjoy; the rest is by the way. I play and I play and I play; then I pick up the pieces and see how I did. It's only at that moment that I realize I was playing for real money. How could I play at all if I started thinking about the sums involved? Can you measure the goods and services a ten-thousand-dollar bet is going to buy? No. But you can measure the intrinsic feeling you get from gambling. Everybody has these subtle energies floating around inside. Some people get through their whole lives sublimating them, repressing them. But there are gamblers here who don't sublimate them; they let them out. That's what high rolling is about."

54

The Sombrero Room is as far from community centers in the slums as the poker games that Appleman now plays are from the quarter-and-fifty-cents-limit games in which he started, "where fifty dollars was a fortune." It is also a long way from the analyst's consulting room, although *sublimation* is a word much favored by Freudians when they discuss gambling. Appleman, however, is using it without any narrow, disapproving psychoanalytic connotations; the sublimation he is talking about is a passport to freedom from the choking constrictions of self. W. H. Auden once wrote of a young poet, "One has the impression that, on returning from a walk, [the inhabitants of his poems] could tell one more of what they had worried about than of what they had seen." Poker was Appleman's way out of worry into alertness and objectivity. When he said, "Gambling is a romance," he was not referring to the smoke-filled rooms, the sullen tribal faces, or the stilted backchat that passes for conversation; he meant the art of the game at its highest level and the romance of personal liberty.

It is a romance that mesmerizes all the high rollers. They pride themselves on the fact that they survive spectacularly well outside the system: no bosses or government bureaucrats on their backs telling them what they should do and how they should do it, no routine that is not of their own choosing, no success that is not the result of their own unaided talents. Also no failure. They are mesmerized by the romance of big losses as much as by that of big wins, and are not interested in compromise. Jack Binion told me of one old-timer who, like all serious gamblers, had been broke more times than he could count. But at the age of seventy-three he had one final lucky streak and found himself $700,000 ahead. Everyone — even the other gamblers — told him to buy himself an annuity policy. A hundred thousand dollars would assure him of a good living for the rest of his life and leave him $600,000 to gamble with. "But he didn't even consider it," Binion said. "He would rather take his chances of going broke. Which he did, and it didn't bother him at all. And, when you think about it, he was right. If you go broke here in America, you don't really starve to death. From the financial point of view, there is a far greater difference between you and some poor native in Africa than there is between you and the richest man in the world. We all eat much the same food and sleep on the same brand of mattress as the Hunt brothers down there in Dallas. This shirt of mine is one hundred percent cotton, and that's all Bunker Hunt is going to be able to wear. So maybe he can take a private jet while I have to stay home. But that's no big deal. Once you reach the lower middle class in the United States, there is no great difference between the top and the bottom. Here at the Horseshoe, if these guys go broke they are going to have to play cheaper. That's the only difference."

"Cheaper?" I said. "There are fortunes changing hands every day."

Binion shook his head. He seemed disappointed in me. We had appeared to be understanding each other, but now, as though for the first time, he registered my English accent and realized that, after all, I was just another uncomprehending foreigner. "In the free enterprise system, you have to assume that each guy is the best judge of what he does with his own money," he explained patiently. "I've often thought, If I got really hungry for a good milk shake, how much would I pay for one? People will pay a hundred dollars for a bottle of wine; to me that's not worth it. But I'm not going to say it is foolish or wrong to spend that kind of money, if that is what you want. So if a guy wants to bet twenty or thirty thousand dollars in a poker game, that is his privilege. Society might consider it bad judgment, but if that is what he wants to do, you can't fault him for it. That's America." And that, too, is Las Vegas — the only place on earth where they justify gambling as a form of patriotism.

4

THE rooms in the Golden Nugget are supposed to remind you of the frontier days. The crimson walls are hung with prints of Wild West scenes, featuring cowboys, gamblers, and ladies of easy virtue; the crimson velvet curtains at the windows and the bedhead are draped with tasseled golden cords; the bed itself, the size of a football field, has an ornate "GN" embroidered in gold, like Napoleon's coat of arms, at the center of its heavy crimson cover; there are lace curtains behind the velvet at the windows. But the attempted delusion ends there. The view is of parking lots, a shabby back-street hotel for real losers, a couple of shops offering LOANS in letters as big as their storefronts, then railroad tracks and, beyond, the blank buff desert ringed with bluish mountains.

For half an hour each evening, about six, the sunlight floods in from the west, creating an illusion of out-of-doors, although the windows do not open and the hum of the air conditioning rises angrily with the intrusion of natural light.

Downstairs is all polished mahogany and brass, fake Tiffany lamps, and the style of instant friendliness that Westerners have adopted as their own. "Hi! How are you?" calls the occupant of the room next to mine when the Oriental waiter wheels in his breakfast trolley at midday. And the waiter answers with an un-Oriental "Hi! How are *you*?"

So why does the prospect of four weeks in this pleasant hotel seem at times like a prison sentence? Because time has been annihilated in this city without clocks, because there is no fresh air and nowhere to go except the casino. By ten in the morning, the heat is merciless, and in 1981 the Golden Nugget had no pool. When I forced myself to take a walk — five blocks across to Garces, five blocks up to Eighth Street, five blocks across again to Fremont, then back past the souvenir shops to the hotel — I returned sweating, feet swollen, mouth parched, as though I had just spent a bad half hour in a prison recreation yard. After a week in Glitter Gulch, I began to exhibit symptoms of physical deprivation — nervous tension, disorientation, insomnia, loss of appetite — which seemed inappropriate in a town geared exclusively to self-indulgence.

Later, I discovered the little swimming pool at the top of the Mint, just across from the Golden Nugget and next door to the Horseshoe. Every afternoon at five, I sneaked up there for an hour and plodded up and down in the overheated water under the giant illuminated figures of the only clock visible anywhere downtown. Afterward, I lay in the harsh sun, listening to the television aerials creak in the wind, or walked the perimeter of the roof and admired the town spread out below, its signs neutralized by the sunlight, and the ring of folded mountains edging the horizon. At that hour, there were rarely more than three or four people around the pool, and often I had the place to myself except for the sand-colored desert birds hopping about among the aerials and the bored attendant waiting to close the doors at six. Silence, fresh air, physical release, and space: I felt like a prisoner reprieved.

There were people in town who felt the same, though for different reasons. "Sure, I'm from Texas, but I cain't go back there." Tony Salinas is a heavily built, handsome man with long black hair and a slightly olive Mexican complexion. He lounged at a poker table in a break between games, very much at his ease. "I got me into a hassle with the FBI," he said. "You see, I've always liked to gamble real high. I got a flair for handicapping football games — in 1980 I won me the World Championship NFL Football Handicapping Contest — and the feds reckoned I was making a book. It warn't true, but they leaned on me all the same. When they found they couldn't hang a charge on me, they tried to get me to snitch on other gamblers down there in San Antonio, and when I wouldn't do that they got mad. They started this case that dragged on for six years. Finally, the judge said, 'Mr. Salinas, I don't want you and the FBI playing cops and robbers no more. I'm going to fine you ten thousand dollars and give you five years in prison.'"

"For gambling?"

"Right. It's a victimless crime, but it ain't legal in Texas. But the judge knew that was the way I made my living, so he made me an offer. 'Pay that fine,' he said, 'and I'll give you sixty days to move yourself and your family to Nevada. Gambling is legal out there, and that's where you should be. You do that and I'll change the prison sentence to five years' probation.' 'Judge,' I said, 'I've been wanting to go to Nevada for six years, but you ain't let me leave Texas on account of this case.' 'Well, I'm letting you now,' he said. 'Just so you don't come back here for five years.' I'm no dummy. He knew I'd say yes. An offer I couldn't refuse, right?"

"You mean he sentenced you to five years in Las Vegas?"

"Right. I moved here on July 28, 1978, and everything's been just great for me since then. My first year, I got very lucky and won a million dollars. I ain't never going back."

Because gambling is officially illegal in so many other states, even the most respectable Nevada professionals often find themselves at odds with the law. On the penultimate evening of the tournament, when all the contests had been settled except the ten-thousand-dollar buy-in hold 'em prize, which decides who will be next World Champion, there was a prize giving in the Sombrero Room. All the previous World Champions were present except Bryan "Sailor" Roberts, who won the title in 1975. "Sailor can't be with us this evening," Jack Binion explained, "because he's in jail just now." The audience murmured sympathetically. Binion went on, "But don't worry. He'll be back tomorrow." Polite applause.

Cowboy Wolford, another top player, was unable to

take part in the tournament at all. Pinned to the back wall of a small annex to the Sombrero Room where poker is played away from the din of the main casino was a message from him expressing his sincerest regrets. Apparently, when Cowboy wins big he tips everyone in sight — the dealers, the cocktail waitresses, the old blacks who sweep the cigarette butts from the floor. The previous year, he took a spectacularly large pot in a side game and, in his elation, tipped the man standing next to him. But the man standing next to him was from the Internal Revenue Service, and he thought he was being offered a bribe. Byron "Cowboy" Wolford is now serving thirty days.

Few of the poker players, however, are as headlong in their dealings with the law. They usually handle its representatives as subtly as they handle each other during the games. One of the professionals was once called before a grand jury investigating a mobster. "You know him?" he was asked.

The poker player shrugged and said, "We've played cards together."

"Did he talk to you?"

"He talked some."

"What did he say?"

"The usual things: 'Check,' 'Raise,' but mostly 'Take 'em.' "

For those who live on less exalted levels, the advice is simple: "Don't mess with the heat." In Las Vegas, the heat comes in many forms and uniforms, and all of it, they say, is "very heavy." The Las Vegas Police Department is responsible for Glitter Gulch and the rest of the city; the Strip is Clark County and belongs to the Sheriff's Department; each casino has its own private army of security men, wearing its own special uniform. In their different styles, they all contribute to the spectacle.

One afternoon, for example, there was an LVPD patrol car double-parked at the corner outside the Golden Nugget. An emaciated man with cropped gray hair stood in front of it, stripped to the waist, leaning forward with his hands on the hood. His face was as lipless as a skeleton's, and he had no eyebrows. A dirty red shirt lay on the hood of the car, the contents of his pockets beside it: scraps of paper, a filthy handkerchief, a few coins, a billfold, a green comb. Two huge policemen were searching him methodically and with distaste; a third sat in the car typing information into a small computer between the front seats. All three had mustaches, beer bellies, big revolvers, and a great deal of creaking leather. One of them, grimacing, slid his hand inside the emaciated man's waistband, found something, and then — fastidiously, as though not wishing to soil his fingers — unbuttoned and unzipped his jeans and pulled them down a few inches. Underneath was a second pair of trousers, dirty gray. The emaciated man gave the policeman his lipless grin and shrugged helplessly. The two giants began to empty the pockets of the inner trousers: two battered billfolds and something that looked like an airplane ticket. They laid these on the hood of the patrol car, alongside the other bits and pieces and the red shirt. While this was happening, a crowd of garishly dressed tourists drew slowly closer. "Got yourself an audience at last," said one of the policemen. The emaciated man laughed ingratiatingly, ducking his head sidewise, hands still flat on the hood. The policeman inside the patrol car went on punching information into his computer. The gawking crowd closed in.

Whatever his prospects, the emaciated man was lucky not to have been picked up by one of the private armies. A thief who was caught rifling a bedroom in the Horseshoe was hauled by the guards into their special room on the second floor and beaten so severely that his yells, I was told, could be heard not only in the casino but also clear across the street. The Horseshoe does not have a problem with theft.

The other casinos are more philosophical. One afternoon, I left a gold cigarette lighter by the pool at the top of the Mint, and by the time I realized that it was gone the pool was closed. Late that night, I reported the loss to the Mint's security guards, who wrote it all down in laborious detail and did nothing at all. The next day, the young pool attendant returned the lighter to me; he had found it when he was putting the sun chairs away. But he had not bothered to inform security, and they had not bothered to ask him. Tourists come and go but good staff is hard to find.

The previous summer, I spent a weekend at one of the most sedate casinos, with my wife and two children. While I played cards, they sunbathed and swam. On the second afternoon, my wife came back to the bedroom to find all the money gone from her purse. The head of security was overweight and melancholy. "Nothing we can do about it," he said.

"It had to be someone with a passkey."

"You know how many people we got working in this place, lady? Pushing two thousand is how many. You know how many passkeys there are?"

"One of the maids barged in this morning while I was in the shower. When I opened the door, she ran out as if I'd caught her at something." My wife was so angry she was having difficulty holding back her tears. She blew her nose and said, "I could recognize her."

"Wouldn't do no good." The security man patted the air between them benevolently. "How you going to prove it's your money she got? Even if you left your purse lying there on the bed and hid in the bathroom while they stole it, you still couldn't nail 'em. They call that entrapment. Ain't nothing no good. I've known guests here, they hide their diamonds in the toilet tank and lose 'em all the same. Anything valuable, you take it with you or deposit it at the front desk."

My wife blew her nose again. "It's outrageous."

"Sure is." He nodded placidly. "But you got insurance, right? So let's you and I fill in a report and you claim it all back."

The guard was unruffled, and not just because he was bored and powerless. He knew that sooner or later everything finds its way back into the gambling economy: jewelry, cameras, lighters, pens as well as money. All of it gets sold or pawned, then comes back as chips or small change in the slots.

"Las Vegas is like a parasite that feeds on money," said a man from Texas. "It sits here in the middle of the desert and produces absolutely nothing, yet it supports half a million people. It depends on the rest of the United States to feed it money, which it channels through the casinos to those five hundred thousand people. I guess it's a kind of modern miracle, something like the loaves and the fishes. I see the casinos packed with tourists telling themselves they are having a good time losing their money, and it's beyond my comprehension. Yet they're always full."

"And you continue to come."

"Poker is how I make my living. And I approve of the location. The desert cuts Vegas off from the real world. You have to make an effort to come here, you have to have money to lose. If the casinos were in a metropolitan area, the people who couldn't afford to lose — construction workers, taxicab drivers, housewives, mail clerks — would gamble because the opportunity was there. In Vegas, suckers are suckers by choice. Without them, there wouldn't be a gambling economy." He glanced at his watch and rose to his feet. "Time to play." He paused, glanced at me quickly, and looked away, as though embarrassed. "One thing," he said. "That stuff about the parasite."

I waited.

"Don't use my name. I'd hate anyone to think I was bad-mouthing the old place."

IN the first years of the World Series of Poker, everything about the occasion was amateur except the players. Word went around, although no one was actually invited, and the events were not even scheduled. "If seven seven-card stud players arrived at the Horseshoe at the same time, they'd play the seven-stud contest — provided one of them wasn't asleep," Eric Drache told me. Despite the haphazardness, the event grew steadily, and after five years Jack Binion asked Drache to organize it for him. "I don't take a fee," Drache said. "Jack has done me so many favors I could do this for the rest of my life and still be in his debt. Anyway, I like organizing things."

Now a schedule is sent out a couple of months in advance to a mailing list of players all over the world; there are thirteen separate events; a public-relations firm from Los Angeles issues daily press releases, and they are regularly picked up by the wire services; television cameras film the highlights of the main events; even the London *Times* and *Observer* carry the results.

Meanwhile, the players keep on coming. By 1981, the number of experts willing to put up a ten-thousand-dollar stake to compete for the title of World Hold 'Em Champion had grown from the original six to seventy-five. There were at least a couple of hundred aspirants for the other titles, and still more who came to the Horseshoe simply for the side games that are played day and night while the tournament is in progress.

By late afternoon on May 5, the end of the second week of the World Series, only two players remained of twenty-seven who had anted $5000 each — plus a fifty-dollar buy-in for table time and dealers — to enter the seven-card high (limit) world championship. Johnny Moss, Doyle Brunson, Puggy Pearson, and Stu Ungar had all been eliminated on the first day. Other big names — Chip Reese, Bobby Baldwin — had followed them during the second morning, and only Eric Drache and A. J. Myers were left for a final showdown under the inhumanly bright lights set up by the television crew.

Their appearance suggested that they had reached a secret agreement to stage the game as a confrontation between the East Coast and the West. Myers's patterned shirt was open halfway to his navel, showing gray chest hair and a heavy gold chain around his neck. His straw hat with the wide scarlet band printed with white flowers was tilted at a rakish angle, his half-glasses were perched on the end of his nose, and he was chewing a gigantic cigar. A second cigar, wrapped in cellophane, lay on the table beside his stacked chips. Eric Drache, in contrast, was a model of Eastern discretion: subdued sports jacket of herringbone Harris tweed, Viyella shirt, sober woolen tie. He looked more like an Oxford don than like a gambler. He also looked bored.

"I feel I'm anteing myself to death," he had said to me a couple of days before. "If they made a film of my life, half the footage would be of my hand throwing in ante after ante after ante. As if it had a life of its own, like Dr. Strangelove's. And every ante is one step closer to the grave. O.K., I'm winning at the moment, so it's easy to enjoy it, because I can kid myself that I will use the money for something more interesting than poker, like travel. But I won't, of course, and I wonder where this is going to end. I'm never going to have a job now. I mean, who is going to pay me three hundred thousand dollars a year? I'm at the top of my profession, and there aren't many opportunities at the top. I'd probably be good in public relations, but I'm not prepared to start at the bottom and work my way up — even if I had the qualifications. So poker is my only security. Some security, though Johnny Moss is a great inspiration: seventy-four years old, still playing every day, and still winning. Even so, I'm thirty-eight now, and I wouldn't want to think my next thirty or forty years are going to be spent in a poker game. I've already been playing professionally for twenty years. In the same game, really. I mean, how long is a poker game? If you play for a living, there is no end to it. Just because it breaks up doesn't mean it ends. The players may go away, but they are still thinking about it, replaying hands, working out their strategy. And they'll be there again the next day. Them or someone else.

"It's utterly unproductive. You can't even carry on a conversation. The losers say, 'Shut up and deal,' and anyway how much input can there be with guys who play twelve hours, then go home and sleep? What's happened to them? What are they going to talk about? Their dreams? A few years back, there was one old guy, a regular, who didn't even know there was a war on in Vietnam. That's why we all enjoy it when someone comes in from out of town. But we don't get many of them, because the game is too high.

"So we have our family of Vegas professionals. Part of the tension of the game is not created by the size of the stakes; it's a family tension, a terrible intimacy. It's like being stir crazy, doing time with the same seven guys in a cell day after day. If someone told me I had to go to the Horseshoe and play for forty-eight hours straight, I'd wonder what I'd done wrong that merited two days in jail. You're just stuck there. There's nothing to see, and, for me, there's not even that much interest in the game anymore. I've seen it all before. Everything that could happen has happened: I've fallen asleep in the middle of a deal; I've played an entire hand without being dealt any hole cards. I've not yet had a guy die on me at the table, though others have. Apart from that, you name it. I've seen it.

"I would willingly pay a hundred dollars a day to have a news ticker go by, so I'd have something to occupy my mind. As it is, I try to manufacture interest. Sometimes I pick up my cards and look at all three at once. Sometimes I squeeze them very slowly to keep myself in suspense. Sometimes, if I'm drawing to a flush, I arch them up so that the upper card reflects on the back of the lower; then I can tell whether it's black or red and narrow my chances down to even money. Anything to alleviate the boredom. I look at every pretty girl who passes, and every well-dressed guy. That's not good for my poker; you're supposed to concentrate. But I'm so bored I do it anyway."

Drache had been tired that day, after a long poker session constantly interrupted by people bringing him problems about the tournament and its organization. The voice of the switchboard operator intoning "Telephone call for Eric Drache, telephone call for Eric Drache" was a continual ground bass to the din of the casino. He was probably also tense about the imminent seven-stud competition, in which his professional reputation would be at stake. But now he had made it to the final showdown, and he seemed bored again, despite the occasion, despite the money involved, despite the overwhelming competitive urge to win. When all was said and done, it was just another poker game.

Drache and Myers lounged nonchalantly in their chairs and made jokes to each other sotto voce. The television producer fussed around them irritably, trying to create the impression of seriousness and strain he considered appropriate to the worth of the chips — $135,000 — divided between them on the table. He gestured to the camera and sound men to close in on Drache. Drache grinned at the tournament's floor manager, an old friend from the game in New Jersey. Speaking clearly for the benefit of the microphone probing the air above his left shoulder, he said, "If I lose two pots in a row, Frank, call time out." Then he ducked down, took a Kleenex from a box beneath the table, and wiped his forehead. The television producer signaled brusquely to his cameraman to switch to Myers.

Drache leaned back and said to me, "In the last year, I've spent more time with A.J. than I have with my wife."

Myers nodded cheerfully while his wife and his daughter, the odalisque, sitting behind him, smiled their approval.

Drache was probably not exaggerating. He and Myers seemed to know each other's game so intimately that they might as well have been playing with all the cards exposed. Drache bet on an open pair of aces — a very strong hand — but when Myers raised him back, showing nothing higher than an eight, he folded immediately.

"Pity," said Myers, and turned over his hole cards: two more eights.

"Surprise, surprise," said Drache.

The cards were not running for Drache, and Myers was "on a rush," hitting hand after hand, as if by magic. There was nothing Drache could do except endure it stoically, retrench, risk nothing, and hope that his chances would come before the antes ate him up.

"It's a war of attrition," he said. "And it's costing me seven hundred dollars a hand." But he did not seem perturbed.

In seven-card stud, each player is dealt two cards face down at the start and one card face up. According to Vegas rules, which were drawn up to promote action by getting the players committed to the pot, "the low man brings it in" — that is, the player with the lowest exposed card has to bet. Three more cards are then dealt face up, with a round of betting after each, initiated by the player with the highest exposed cards. The seventh card is then dealt face down, and there is a final round of betting.

For six consecutive deals, Drache was forced to bring it in, Myers raised immediately, Drache folded. Myers half turned to his wife and daughter and the railbirds massed behind them. He arched his eyebrows, turned out his palms, and said, around his cigar, "This man plays poker for a living, would you believe it?" Drache laughed along with everyone else, but was not taken in: he knew better than anyone that the wisecracks were a form of pressure, keeping him on the defensive.

Finally, Drache won a hand. "Watch it," he announced. "I'm on a rush." He won the next hand, too, but then began folding again.

"End of rush," said Myers.

For two hours, the game dragged on uneventfully, and then it flared briefly to life for one hand. On the sixth card, Drache was showing a nine, a deuce, and a pair of fours, and had two more nines in the hole, giving him a full house. Myers was showing a jack, a seven, and a pair of fives; he had a second jack in the hole, giving him two pairs. But when Myers bet after the seventh card Drache did not raise him. Correctly. Myers's last card was another jack, giving him a higher full house.

After that, it was only a matter of time before Drache was frozen out — "like Broomcorn's uncle," as they say in Texas, chewed up by the antes. Twenty minutes later, he "went down to the river" (took all seven cards) on an open-ended straight, nine to the queen, and did not make it. Myers took the hand and the championship with aces up. His prize money was $67,500, Drache's $27,000.

Within a couple of hours, they were facing each other again across the poker table, but for much higher stakes than were allowed in the official championship.

6

MARIO PUZO, who loves Las Vegas, thinks that three days is the ideal time to spend in the town. If you get lucky sooner, get out on the next plane, since the casinos make their two-billion-dollar annual profit out of one simple certainty: nobody stays lucky.

Puzo plays casino games in Vegas — baccarat, roulette, craps, blackjack — where the house's edge, the 2 to 16 percent permanently in its favor, will always eat up the gambler in the long run. Poker, even in Las Vegas, is a less one-sided struggle. Although the casinos either charge an hourly rate for one's seat or cut a small sum from each pot, the real money changes hands between the players. That is why most of the poker rooms are off to one side, away from the main action; the managements do what they can to discourage high rollers from losing their thousands to a poker player instead of throwing it off at craps or roulette. That is also why the poker professionals are the only gamblers who seem to survive the town, provided they can avoid the temptation to destroy their winnings in other, less predictable forms of gambling.

Most of them, incidentally, are banned from the blackjack tables; the casinos assume that if they can play poker at the highest level, they either must have a photographic memory for cards or can easily master one of the counting systems by which the blackjack player is able to beat the odds. Eric Drache, for instance, was barred the first time he tried to play the game. He knew nothing about it but was betting heavily, because that is how he always bets. He had lost $5000 in less than an hour, and then the shift changed. The new pit boss recognized him and immediately stopped the game. "This man gambles for a living," he said. "He can't play here."

"He didn't know I knew nothing about the game and had no chance of winning," Drache told me. "But that was fine by me. It gave me the opportunity to ask myself what I was doing there anyway. I've never played blackjack since."

The poker professionals also survive because they spend so much time in Vegas that they are impervious to seductions that outsiders find hard to handle: the seduction of the action that never stops, and surrounds you wherever you go (there are girls in miniskirts and plunging décolletages selling keno tickets in the restaurants while you eat and at the poolside while you sunbathe, and, in fact, everywhere except on the tennis courts and the golf courses); the seduction of the movie-star image that the casinos project onto their guests (the suites of rooms with vast, draped beds, sunken baths of fake marble, twin dressing tables, his and hers, with lights all round the mirrors, just like the makeup rooms in a Hollywood studio); above all, the seductive fantasies of power, stoked high by the fantasies of money and chance.

An example: Joel first arrived in Las Vegas four years ago. It was also his first visit to America, and he was there — like thousands of other Englishmen in that brief interlude when the pound was strong and the dollar weak — because America had unexpectedly become the ideal place for a cheap family holiday. So Joel, his wife, and their children did the grand tour: they admired the view from the top of the Empire State Building and the imperial glories of Washington; they drove across the Golden Gate Bridge, visited Disneyland and Universal City and Marineland; they spent a weekend in Las Vegas; they gawked at the Grand Canyon; and then they homed with relief onto the Fontainebleau in Miami. In Vegas, they stayed at Caesars Palace, and while his wife and children swam, Joel played a little blackjack, a little poker. Since he also played regularly and competently in London, he got out of town without having done himself much harm.

Joel had one peculiarity: at home in the evenings, he never read, he never talked, he never even watched television; he just sat, staring at nothing in particular, puffing a Groucho Marx cigar. "Maybe he was plotting how to sell another dress," said a friend. "For a chap in such a small way of business, he did O.K." Perhaps. But more probably he was letting his fantasies spin, for Joel was cursed with a childish imagination and the inability to distinguish its workings from reality. To anyone who would listen, he invariably reported large poker losses as small wins, small wins as fortunes. He lived in a world of make-believe, presumably because the real world gave him so little to boast about. Since his teens, he had worked in the garment trade for a domineering father who had forced him, at the age of twenty-one, into an old-fashioned arranged marriage with the daughter of a business acquaintance. A year before the American holiday, Joel had finally broken free and set himself up in a small business of his own. The holiday, in fact, was to celebrate the first anniversary of his successful independence.

A childish imagination in a middle-aged body is the ideal formula for what John Gregory Dunne called that "idiot Disneyland with lights" — Las Vegas. Over the years, in London, the only time Joel ever went to the theater was when Frank Sinatra was in town to give one of his special performances. He booked months in advance and took his wife, both of them dressed to kill, in the dutiful spirit in which he went to synagogue for the High Holidays. He always had a couple of spare tickets to sell, at a modest profit, over the poker table. Sinatra was singing at the Palace during Joel's weekend in Vegas, and Joel, his wife, and children sat there enthralled two nights in a row. It seemed to him an obscure sign, a portent: "Las Vegas, Las Vegas, you're my kind of town." Like was calling to like, and continued to call irresistibly during the months of married wrangling after Joel and his family returned to their dreary London suburb. He had raised a little capital for his new business, using his home as collateral, so, for the first time in his life, money was not a problem. He even began to do well in the London poker games, at which he had for years been one of the "providers." The siren call of Vegas became stronger. In November, he returned.

But Joel had not spent all those years of hard graft in the rag trade for nothing. He wanted to go back in style, and he also wanted to go back with the least possible expense to himself. So he arranged a twenty-thousand-dollar line of credit with Caesars Palace. "Not to gamble," he said. "Just to play poker. But in that town you've got to have status." Naturally, the hotel treated him as it treats any customer who indicates that he has a respectable amount to lose: like a king. He was provided, free of charge, with an elegant suite — a circular bed, sunken bath, drinks on the sideboard in the sitting room, a bird's-eye view of the swimming pool. He was bowed to, smiled at, coddled and flattered, wined and dined with the compliments of the management, and provided, also courtesy of the management, with an obliging lady friend. This was a man who had spent his whole adult life with a woman with whom he had scarcely exchanged a civil word, let alone a civil touch, and who was still too terrified of his father ever to risk being caught out in an affair. No matter that the Las Vegas woman was large and raw-boned, with peroxide hair and spangles on her glasses, the fifth of eight children of a security guard from Texarkana; she treated him as regally as everyone else at Caesars Palace did, feigned enthusiasm, and knew how to make him feel manly after a lifetime of subjugation and worthlessness. Belatedly, he discovered the pleasures of sex. He went around in a daze, watching her greedily and with wonder, as if she had just invented the wheel. His fantasies spun more dizzily than ever. At the age of forty-six, he had finally, he decided, fallen in love, but with the desperation of middle age, knowing this might be his last chance. He bought her a hideous gold bracelet and a blue Pontiac Firebird and asked her to marry him. She refused, of course, but in such a way as to leave the door ajar, since a good mark is hard to find, particularly in Las Vegas. Worse still, the confidence she gave him rubbed off at the poker table; he came out winning a few hundred dollars, he claimed, and that meant he did not lose much.

And it finished him. He went back to London, left his wife, and set himself up in an apartment he could not afford. He telephoned the girl in Las Vegas every day and sent her $500 a week, so that she would not need to work. She shared the money with her pimp and continued to do business as usual. Two months later, Joel returned, hoping to make money at the tables. He lost. Once again, he asked her to marry him; once again, she refused. "At least change your job," he pleaded. "Go to dealers' school. I'll pay." His doggedness exasperated her, but she was not a bad-hearted girl. "Joel," she said, patting his thin hair gently, "you peddle schmattes, I peddle pussy. *That's* my job."

Joel flew back to London, sold what was left of his business, returned to Las Vegas, found another blond hooker — this one from Lubbock, Texas — and went through the whole performance again. He also kept on losing, although all he could talk about was his broken heart. It was pure Vegas magic: in less than a year Joel had been transformed from a walk-on uncle in *Goodbye, Columbus* into a tormented Dostoevskian, weeping helplessly on the sofa while his whore tore up bank notes and threw them on the fire. He seemed curiously elated by the role, high on his own disasters. He embraced Vegas as the early Christian martyrs embraced their gridirons: it was his fate, his justification, his fantasy of fantasies. Back in London again, he boasted about his misfortune, claiming he had been set up by the mob: when they heard of his credit at Caesars, he claimed, they sent the girls after him and took a hefty percentage of the money and presents he showered them with. When the girls held back, he added, they were given cement overcoats and dumped in Lake Mead.

Then Joel himself disappeared, trailing bad debts, including an unpaid bill for £750 for telephone calls from London to Las Vegas. Nobody thought to blame the mob. He is rumored to be in Johannesburg, but his wife, who has remarried, is not convinced.

* * *

As a fantasist transfixed on his own imagination, Joel was doomed from the start both by the town and by the game. "There can be no self-deception for a poker player," Mickey Appleman said. "You have to be a realist to be successful. You can't think you've played well if you lose consistently. Unless you can judge how well you play relative to the others, you have no chance." Another reason Joel had no chance was that he was unable to disentangle his gambling from his sex life. This is not a muddle that the professional players ever allow themselves. Nearly all are married to women who, with varying degrees of difficulty, have made their peace with the problems of living with an addict: the vacillation between feast and famine, the long absences while their husbands are on the road, "driving the white line" from game to game, or the different, more complex absence of someone who is physically present while his whole attention is elsewhere. "It takes a special sort of woman to handle marriage to a professional poker player," Bobby Baldwin said. "She has to know she can't change him. She marries him the way he is, with certain habits, certain things he's accustomed to, and she has to learn to live with them." Baldwin is usually as sensitive and delicate as a young girl in his attitude toward people, scrupulously polite, scrupulously modest, but on this topic his voice was as steely as it was at the poker table, without a flicker of apology. "As I see it, if a man is not allowed to live his life the way he sees fit, then he's with the wrong person. You can't sacrifice your life just because someone gives you a me-or-it ultimatum. And that cuts both ways, of course. I've been married twice. I loved my first wife very much, but she just couldn't cope with the lifestyle of a gambler. Shirley, my second wife, seems to like it. I was very lucky to find her."

Shirley Baldwin is a small-town version of Jacqueline Onassis: bouffant hair, round face, small features, a diamond as big as the Ritz. Like the other wives, she sometimes watches her husband play in important games, sitting glumly through the long hours of monotony and stilted conversation, ready to smile encouragement or respond to a private joke when something like that is required, as patient as a nun and as devoted. But more often the wives keep away from the casinos, carrying on with their lives and their families as if poker were just a profession like any other. Virgie Moss and Louise Brunson keep an eye on the family investments and the day-to-day finances, worry about the children, make sure their husbands have clean laundry and proper meals, and never ask about wins or losses but know how to be appreciative or sympathetic, as the situation demands.

Some of the younger wives are, predictably, less bound by the traditional domestic role; Jane Drache, for instance, is studying for a B.A. at Columbia, and her husband has seen to it that she is financially secure in her own right. "I want our marriage to be based on our relationship, not on money," he said. "She can leave me any time she wants, and it won't be a monetary decision." But the Draches are New Yorkers among the Texans, exceptions in a world of old-fashioned male bravado. "Women's all right," said Amarillo Slim. "Only place in the world you can beat one and not get thrown in jail is at the poker table."

Whatever part the wives play, they provide their husbands with a base, a stable point in a notoriously shifting world. "Family and wife and kids give you a foundation," Bobby Baldwin said. "They give you the motivation to be strong and solid, to have backbone, heart, fortitude, or whatever you want to call it. They give you a purpose in life. Without that, it would be hard to control yourself in this business, because if you had no responsibilities, what would it matter if you won or lost? I myself get a big kick out of spoiling my wife and family — and that includes my parents, my grandmother, my brothers. Some of the guys out here know nothing but the gambling world. Well, that's all right, except I think they miss out on the best part of life. Me, I stop to smell the roses."

Mickey Appleman, too, stops to smell the roses, New York style; that is, he reads a great deal, practices meditation, thinks hard about his life and what he is doing with it. On the subject of family, he agrees with Baldwin, but wistfully and from the other side of the fence. "A lot of the guys have someone to go back to," he says. "That security is a source of strength in poker; it helps them win. Me, I'm single. When I finish playing, I go up to my room and, like, I'm alone with myself. So, in a way, it's harder."

Yet Appleman is alone by choice, since, as even Joel discovered, there is no shortage of friendly women in Vegas. The high-stakes poker games always have their groupies loitering at the edges, attracted by the aphrodisiacs of big money and risk. But the atmosphere at Binion's during the poker tournament, despite all the din and razzle-dazzle and tough talking, is strangely sexless. For five weeks each year, the place becomes a world of men without women. Or, rather, the women are there but — except for the few who sit down to play the men on equal terms — only as color in the background, like the voice of the hotel operator over the intercom or the rattle of chips. There is no trace at all of the sensual charge that usually bristles in the air of a holiday resort. The women who do connect seem to spend most of the time listening morosely to passionate but obscure accounts of how some freak tried to run a bluff with a pair of sixes: "I mean, what's two lousy sixes?" The women smile and nod and glance furtively around for relief.

One evening, I was in the elevator of the Golden Nugget with a tall middle-aged cowboy with the aquiline profile and fierce beard of a Spanish conquistador — a man who that afternoon, in true conquistador fashion, had been destroying the nonprofessional hold 'em event. I had seen him seated unmoving behind two gigantic towers, one of black hundred-dollar chips, the other of gray five hundreds capped with three blacks. Each tower was over a foot high and perfectly symmetrical, rising from a base of three chips set side by side. They looked like giant space-age architectural fantasies built in Lego by a patient child — appropriately, patience being what the game is about. But the tournament was over for the day, and now the cowboy was ascending majestically to his room with an Anita Loos blonde in a low-cut pink dress and very high heels, who held a drink in one hand, a cigarette in the other. She hummed "Nowhere Man" to herself and smiled vaguely while the elevator rose and he analyzed for me a key hand I had watched him play. He seemed utterly unaware of her. "When he raises in an early position," he was saying, "I have to read him for nothing better than ace-jack." The elevator stopped, the doors slid apart. The blonde started forward, then hesitated. He raised his hand like a traffic cop, pressed the button to hold the doors open, and continued, "Two aces, two kings, ace-king, he'd have sent it around in the hope of getting in a reraise." Then he moved courteously aside, bowing slightly to the girl as she stepped out in front of him. As the doors closed again, he took her silently by the arm to guide her down the hall. A couple of hours later, when I came down after a nap, the girl was drinking alone at the bar of the Golden Nugget and he was playing poker again across the road at the Horseshoe.

The little old-fashioned courtesies (he was, after all, a man in his fifties), the silence, the firm, businesslike hand gripping the girl's elbow and guiding her to his room were all part of a formal exchange: sex without sensuality, without even much interest; sex bought as one might buy a drink — as a way of winding down after the tension and concentration of gambling, as a hunger to be assuaged, like other hungers, for a fixed price.

Brothels are legal in Nevada, and sexual hypocrisy is the one vice that Las Vegas has never aspired to. At the bus stops along the Strip, there are give-away newspapers offering every variety of playmates, of both sexes. The bordellos and the call-girl agencies ("No need to leave your hotel room") take full-page spreads with blurred, stylized photographs, credit-card logos, and dreadful double-entendres: "The perfect way to climax your stay in Las Vegas." There are also columns of coy personal ads for freelancers with names like Sherri, Terri, Lori, and Desarya. A topless bar just off the Strip not only has dancing girls to cater to most tastes — one fat, one thin, one tough, one yielding — but also offers to customers who can no longer manage the four steps up from the parking lot to the bar a ramp for wheelchairs. There seems no end to the depression induced in the name of pleasure by the entrepreneurs of Clark County, Nevada, and it spreads outward, to professionals and nonprofessionals alike. "I feel that the women here have been hardened," Mickey Appleman said. "They're not vulnerable, like the women back East. It's like they've had their insides stripped out. I guess it's tragic in its own way, but this town is hard on everybody. It strips away your spirituality. In order to be successful on a continual basis out here, you have to remain nonemotional. But when a gambler is nonemotional, then he becomes detached from the person he really is. That's the basic problem of living in Las Vegas: you become despiritualized."

Despiritualized, depersonalized, one-dimensional: that is how life in any Disneyland must always be. But during the World Series of Poker the atmosphere at Binion's Horseshoe is as unwavering and concentrated as that of an Olympic training camp. I have never seen so many apparently healthy men gathered together in one place for so long with such single-mindedness: no sex, no drink, just the turn of the cards hour after hour and the little thrill of excitement and expectation at each new deal.

One afternoon when I was on the way back from my daily swim, two black hookers and their pimp got into the elevator with me at the Mint. The girls were big and exuberant, the man thin as a whippet, with quick, nervous gestures. All of them were festooned like Christmas trees with necklaces and bangles. One of the girls rubbed her shoulder against mine and asked, "Care for a li'l fun, hon?" She was, I suppose, eighteen years old. I smiled and shook my head and said, "I'm too old for fun." She rolled her eyes at the others and winked meaningfully: "Ah make you feel young again, man." We all laughed, though probably at different jokes, the elevator doors opened on the casino, and the three of them strode off, chattering. Odd, I thought, not even to have been tempted.

But later, when I settled down to the evening's hold 'em session at the Nugget and picked up my first cards, my eyes felt fresh, my heart was beating sweetly, all my senses were alert. As the hooker would have said, I felt young again. Perhaps the Freudians are right, after all, when they talk of gambling as sublimation. In the words of another addict, "Sex is good, but poker lasts longer."

7

OYLE BRUNSON, twice winner of the World Series of Poker, was born in 1933 in Longworth, a tiny farming village in West Texas. His father worked on the land and at the local cotton gin. "We weren't that poor," he told me. "We were maybe above average for our community, in that we had plenty to eat and were never really under financial strain, like some of them. But still we never had an abundance of anything. If there was something extra you wanted, you had to get out and hustle for it — chop cotton or work in the construction industry." Brunson paid for his higher education with an athletic scholarship at Hardin-Simmons, a Baptist college in Abilene. He was the star of the basketball team, selected by a basketball magazine as one of the top college players in the country, and courted by the Minneapolis Lakers. He was also a brilliant miler — the best in Texas when he was in high school, and a possible contender for a place on the Olympic team. "I could just run and run," he said. "I never seemed to get tired."

But Brunson's athletic career came abruptly to an end the summer before he was due to graduate, when he was back home working at the Sweetwater plant of U.S. Gypsum. A huge pile of Sheetrock slid outward while he was unloading it, and snapped his right leg in two places. The leg was in plaster for two years, and his career as a professional athlete was over. He stayed on at Hardin-Simmons to take an M.A. in administrative education, with the aim of one day becoming the principal of a county school, but the only position he was offered was that of a high-school basketball coach, at a salary of $4800 a year. Since he was already making more than that in college poker games, he took a job as a business-machine salesman at five times the salary. It didn't last. There was a poker game in progress in the back room of one of the first offices he called on; he sat down at it, and in three hours had won a month's salary. After that, there seemed only one way to go.

The first time I met Brunson, he was standing with his wife, Louise, by the elevators at the Golden Nugget. Louise is a small, plump, talkative woman in her middle forties, with a round, pleasant face and an open smile, which she uses a lot. While we chatted, Brunson dug around absent-mindedly in his pockets and finally pulled out a large handful of chips, mostly black. Louise cupped her hands to receive them and giggled like a young girl.

"What have I done to deserve this?" she asked. Brunson beamed at her.

Brunson is six feet three inches tall and weighs 282 pounds — 100 pounds more than when he was playing basketball. Most of the extra weight is in his belly and his buttocks, and he is fighting it in a halfhearted way. For a year, he has been on a diet that forbids red meat. Red meat, however, does not seem to be his problem. At the poker table, he gulps down milk drinks topped with whipped cream while the other players sip mineral water. During an afternoon break, he slips into the Sombrero Room, where a lavish buffet, covered by a white cloth, is already laid out for the evening meal. He glances slyly round the room, lifts one corner of the cloth, slides out a large wedge of chocolate cake, and goes out again, munching contentedly. "During the tournament, I eat four or five desserts a day," he confided later. "I just cain't keep away from that table." He smiles sweetly, sucking in his lower lip so that only his upper teeth show. The sweet smile, soft face, and great, portly frame, in its brown sports shirt and trousers flowing like a brown spinnaker, give him the air of the benign medieval abbot of some easygoing monastery. Yet, although his broken leg has left him with a permanent limp, he still plays golf to a single-figure handicap and claims he can outlast anyone except Jack Binion on the tennis court or in the swimming pool. "I know it sounds silly," he said, "but I've been heavy all my life, yet I've never *felt* fat. I cain't run anymore, because of my leg, but I can do most everything anyone else can do. I guess what matters is the mental picture you have of yourself."

For many of the top professionals, poker has become

a substitute for sport — something that they turn to when their physical edge has gone, but that demands the same concentration, skill, and endurance and provides a channel for all their bottled-up competitiveness. "Discipline and stamina are what poker is all about, especially when you're competing with top players in games that go on a long time," said Brunson. "Because of my athletic background, I have a lot of both. Sometimes, when I've been playing for a couple of days, I get into a position where I'm uncomfortable. My leg, say, starts hurting a little bit. But I don't change position. I'll sit there and let it hurt, just as a reminder to make myself play good." Another example, perhaps, of the fortitude that poker players value so highly — a physical equivalent of the stoicism with which, on their way up, they endured the bad runs that wiped out their working capital.

Jack Binion calls the professionals "mental athletes." Certainly, in Brunson's mind, poker and sport are inextricably merged. His father — a sweet-tempered man, of whom Brunson speaks with great affection and who was a secret poker player, talented enough to put another son through college on his winnings — died when Brunson was twenty-five. For the next ten years, Brunson was on the road, traveling from game to game; for six of those ten years he teamed up with Amarillo Slim Preston and Sailor Roberts — a partnership that lasted until their joint six-figure bankroll was wiped out during a disastrous visit to Las Vegas in 1964. He speaks of his road years now as a prizefighter speaks of training camp, with a mixture of pride and dismay. "Those years are just a kind of blur," he says. "I barely remember them. But the only way you develop your poker skills and your sixth sense is by putting in a lot of hours. I once went a whole summer without seeing the sun. I would play all night, then sleep all day; go to bed at dawn, get up at sundown. I guess it was just humanly impossible to put in more hours than I did in those ten years. All I did was play poker and sleep and eat and, once in a while, grab a broad — like going to the grocery store."

That is not strictly accurate. Halfway through the decade, Brunson married, and that same year he almost died. Louise was working as a pharmacist in San Angelo, Texas, and he courted her — between games — for two years, during which she sold him every vitamin in the shop several times over. Because he was nearly thirty years old, she assumed he was married, and at first refused to go out with him. When that hurdle was cleared, there was the problem of his profession. "She asked me what I did, and I told her I was a bookmaker," he said. "She thought I said 'bookkeeper,' so she told her mother I was an accountant." He eventually explained the misunderstanding to her, but does not say whether she ever enlightened her mother.

Four months after they married, in August of 1962, Brunson woke up with a sore throat and a lump on his neck the size of a pea. For three weeks, the local doctor fed him antibiotics, while the lump grew to the size of an egg. At that point, worry turned into panic — particularly since one of Brunson's brothers had recently died of cancer. Doyle and Louise hurried to Fort Worth to consult a specialist. The specialist took one look, made reassuring noises, and operated the next day. The cancer was everywhere — in his stomach, his chest, his neck, and near the base of his brain, and was so heavy and so extensive that it was visible to the naked eye. They sewed him back together and told Louise that it was a question of weeks, not months. She was pregnant by then, and in the hope of keeping him alive long enough to see their child she arranged for further surgery, in Houston. There was no hope of saving him, but at least they might delay the cancer's progress to his brain. The operation lasted eight hours and was successful. More important, when the surgeons opened him up again there was no trace at all of the cancer.

The doctors called it "a spontaneous remission"; they also called it "a miracle." Certainly, there seemed no rational explanation for what had happened. One moment, Brunson had been on the scaffold with the rope around his neck; the next, he was a free man. The two conditions seemed equally unreasonable. Later, Louise discovered that several friends had spoken to their pastors, and entire congregations had been praying for her husband's recovery. She took it as a sign, and has since been vigorously Christian — a force in the local church and deeply involved in foreign missions. Brunson himself reserves judgment; he rarely goes to church, but says, "I was brought up in a Christian home and never saw any reason to change the beliefs they taught me as a child." He is also convinced — if only as a poker player — of the power of ESP.

Despite Brunson's skepticism, the miracles continued. Shortly after their child, a daughter, was born, Louise developed a uterine tumor. A major operation was scheduled, but before it could take place all traces of the tumor had disappeared. She went on to have two more children. Then, when Doyla — the eldest was named after Brunson when it was reckoned that he would not live to see her — was twelve, she developed idiopathic scoliosis, acute curvature of the spine. Specialists were consulted, and alternative measures were considered: a body brace or a steel rod implanted in her spine. The best she could hope for was to be permanently crippled. But Louise consulted a famous faith healer, Katherine Kuhlman, and organized a marathon prayer session. Within two weeks, the child's spine had completely straightened of its own accord — one of only three known instances of the affliction's being cured without surgery.

It is a strange background for a master of one of the most realistic of all disciplines. Brunson acknowledges the strangeness, as he would acknowledge a miracle draw at the card table, but does not comment, although he does express pride in his wife's good works. Of his own miracle, he says, "I never did think I was going to die. Just before I went to Houston for the second operation, my friends gathered from all over to say goodbye, so I took the hint and made out a list of pallbearers. It was real morbid. But in my heart I never believed it. Maybe that was because I was only thirty and at that age dying is something that happens to old people, not to you. Perhaps that attitude helped pull me through. As I see it, death has several stages: the first is disbelief, the last is acceptance. Well, I just refused to accept it. I'd been an athlete, see, and I'd always overcome everything I'd set my mind to. I guess I thought I could overcome death, too." In Brunson's case, physical strength became moral and mental toughness, as though he had decided that if death could not touch him nothing would. "My whole attitude toward life was different from that point on," he told me one day in Vegas. "I really began to enjoy it. Even though I still played poker a lot, I had an appreciation of things I'd never had before. Up until then, I'd just driven the white line from game to game, as if I had blinkers on. Now I began to notice the trees and the flowers and how blue the sky got."

Brunson also went on to an extraordinary winning streak after his recovery: fifty-three straight poker sessions in a row. It was as if nothing could resist the vitality unleashed by his brush with death. By the end of those fifty-three games, he had paid off all his medical bills and had enough left over to keep his family in comfort for years. Since then, he has not looked back.

All that is left of Brunson's cancer is scars on his neck. His face is heavily jowled and is balanced slightly to the left. Under the right jawline, running back toward the ear, is a large indentation covered with grafted skin, like a crater lake skimmed over with ice. A little in front of that is a gigantic L-shaped scar, which he acquired a couple of years ago when surgeons lifted back the skin to cut out another growth — this time, mercifully, a benign lymphatic tumor.

These brutal confrontations with cancer have confirmed Brunson in his belief in himself as a winner, invincible. Death is, quite simply, a matter that no longer concerns him; instead, it seems to have intensified for him the image of himself when he was young. In 1980, he went back to a class reunion at high school, Sweetwater High. This is what he said about it: "Age hasn't meant any-thing to me until very recently; I felt the same at twenty-five and thirty-five and forty. Then I went back to this high-school reunion and saw how everyone else had aged, and I knew I'd aged, too. But I also saw that some of those guys were ready to sit down and die right there. O.K., you can't help how you look physically, provided you take care of yourself. But there we all were, forty-six years old, and some of us were ready to die and others were still youthful, just as they were at school. That made me realize I never want to get old mentally. I'd like to stay like Johnny Moss. He's seventy-four now, and in the last year or two he's begun to look a little older, but he doesn't think old at all. Mentally, he's still a young man: he stays up two or three nights on end playing cards, he thinks about the broads, he has plans for the future. I hope I'll always be that way."

Apart from the scars, the one remaining trace of Brunson's run-in with death is an obsession with punctuality. I discovered this when I arranged to meet him for breakfast at seven o'clock. I was up at a quarter past six, but as I was leaving my room someone called me from New York on business. The call dragged on, and I got to the Sombrero Room twenty minutes late. Brunson was most of the way through his breakfast, and nodded curtly when I sat down, his face shut as tight as a bank vault. Although I apologized, and explained what had happened, he clearly did not believe me. He spoke little, but his irritation seemed to fill the empty restaurant like a fog, and was a long time dispersing. The following morning, the situation was reversed: I was there at seven sharp, he arrived at seven-thirty. When he realized his mistake — he thought we had changed the time — he seemed genuinely shocked, apologized more than was necessary, and returned to the subject later, this time angrily. "To me, a man's word is his bond," he said. "When you say you're going to be somewhere at a certain time, that's your word, and if you don't keep the appointment your word's not worth a damn. I feel very strongly about it."

The previous afternoon, I had watched him count out 200 hundred-dollar bills from the gigantic wad in his pocket and hand them over to another gambler affably, without a sign of annoyance, so I asked, "Why *so* strongly?"

"The most valuable thing I've got is my time," he answered. "It's more valuable to me than money or anything else."

It was the only sign he ever gave of being a man who feels he is living on borrowed time.

We had arranged to meet at such an ungodly — and un-Vegas — hour because for five days, beginning May 4, the Doyle Brunson Invitational Golf Tournament was being held at the tight little course behind the Dunes Hotel, and Brunson took me along to watch. The tournament does not have the approval of the Professional Golfers Association, since their rules specify that the players do not involve themselves in gambling. Brunson grumbled about this all the way out to the course. He was riled by the hypocrisy. "All golfers gamble, even if it's only for a buck or two," he said. "What difference does the scale make?" But he was also riled because a Baptist upbringing dies hard, and he is touchy about the shady public image of his chosen profession. The year before — "1980 was my year of reunions" — he had gone home to Longworth and met his ancient first-grade teacher. She fixed him reproachfully with her pale blue eyes and asked him what he did. He told me, "I said, 'Play poker,' and she just looked at me and shook her head and said, 'My goodness, can't you find something better to do?' " He, too, shook his head, mournfully. "That's the attitude of the whole community," he went on. "They're country people, good people, but they don't understand that there are ways of life different from the ones they are used to, and they won't accept them." To be very rich as well as respected and famous in certain circles yet still to be looked down on by what gamblers call "the straight world" is an irony that Brunson is unable to appreciate.

Despite the PGA, several dozen young golf professionals had entered the tournament, and about the same number of gamblers had gathered for the action. They milled around in the clubhouse while Brunson lumbered out to the first tee and back, to work out the odds. "I watch 'em hit one ball, then I make a lineup," he said. He took notes of the bets on the back of an envelope and paid the winners in cash as soon as the game was over.

Brunson spent a great deal of time that day in consultation with a little man called Billy. Billy had a full head of gray hair, an assertive backside, and a sly satyr's face — eyes sharp and slitted, the corners of his mouth upturned at some permanent secret joke. I heard him say, "I bet ten thousand on each man."

"You like that two-to-one bet, you got it," Brunson answered.

Later, Brunson told me that Billy was "the biggest sports bettor in the world." He sounded respectful, and I wondered how big is big, since Brunson himself once lost $180,000 on a single hole of golf, and often plays for $200,000 or $300,000 a round. "Doyle's played for more in one day than Watson and Nicklaus win in a whole year," a friend of Brunson's had told me.

Out on the course, the sun shone on the dew, and the cool air smelled of cut grass. Birds called sweetly to each other from the tattered palms and junipers. The mountains circling the horizon shimmered in the haze. "That's not haze," said Brunson. "That's pollution." Nevertheless, it seemed a long way from Glitter Gulch.

Most of the regulars from the high-stakes poker games at Binion's were out there to enjoy the fresh air and the action. They buzzed from hole to hole and game to game in white-canopied carts, like a swarm of demented insects. One couple, however, stayed at a sedate and watchful distance: a battered giant, who looked like a middle-aged stand-in for the Incredible Hulk, and a tiny, monkey-faced old man with a heavy Navajo bracelet on one wrist, a gold Patek-Philippe watch on the other, and, on that forearm, a gaudy tattoo of a dancing girl wearing a sombrero. The other gamblers eyed them respectfully from a distance, but during the five days the tournament lasted I never saw the two exchange a word — with each other or with anyone else. When I finally asked Brunson if this odd couple was a Mafia capo and his bodyguard, he refused to be drawn out. "I don't even know for sure if the mob exists," he said. "But out here if you eat a pizza, they think you're tied in with Chicago."

The officials were monitoring the games with two-way radios, and the gamblers continually buzzed up to them to ascertain the state of play elsewhere on the course. Then they would swoop down on Brunson to add to their bets. Billy paused briefly by our cart. "Plus six for twenty," he muttered, and swooped away again. Brunson made a note on the back of his envelope.

Brunson watched critically while one of the players three-putted. As the man walked dejectedly from the green to the next tee, Brunson asked him how he stood. "Three down," the man answered. His scarlet trousers and white sweater seemed inappropriate to his gloom. Brunson patted his shoulder like a fatherly bear. "Don't you worry none," he said. "You're doing just fine." As we drove away, he smiled his sweet smile and shifted his large, soft body contentedly on the cart seat. "That's goo-ood," he said. "I betted on the other guy."

The cool, delectable air and the fun of betting on other people's play seemed to loosen everyone up. Jack Straus drove up to us and launched into one of his innumerable stories. "Remember the time, Doyle, I wanted to take you off to that little island?" Brunson grinned sheepishly and looked away, pretending to watch a distant golfer square up for his approach shot. Straus turned to me, in full flow now. "The idea was, we'd rent a condominium and play golf and fish from early morning to night," he said. "We'd stock the icebox with salads and fruit and fresh vegetables and maybe take off some weight. But Doyle's wife is very religious, and somehow she got the idea we were going down there to chase girls. Well, Doyle was like a ninety-year-old man accused of rape — he wanted to plead guilty. So there was some kind of argument. Finally, I told her that if I was going to try to grab a girl, having Doyle along would be like having a dead chicken hanging round my neck. And that settled it, though we never did go. Right, Doyle?" Brunson nodded cheerfully, sucking his lower lip.

At one of the short holes, Puggy Pearson stood next to Brunson, sizing the players up beadily along a gigantic cigar. The first man drove impeccably, and the ball landed just short of the green. His opponent took a practice swing and addressed his ball.

"How much on him?" Pearson whispered.

"Five to four."

"I'll take a dime of that action" — a dime in Las Vegas parlance being a thousand dollars. The second player swung, the ball soared, faltered, dropped into a bunker. The player rubbed his lower back and began talking to his opponent and an official. Then he turned on his heel, climbed into his cart, and drove off toward the clubhouse. The gamblers clustered around the official; the player, he announced, had pulled a muscle and conceded the game.

"Shee-it," Pearson said.

Brunson pulled out his envelope and scribbled, "Puggy — $1,000."

"That guy," Pearson muttered angrily. "He's got more pooch in him than a cocker spaniel."

"Pooch" or "dog" — short for "underdog" — is gamblers' slang for "loser," and a ruling concept among the high-stakes players. "Doyle Brunson has absolutely no dog in him," an oil man from Albuquerque told me. "He'll make bad matches at golf, he'll play uphill, but he'll shoot out of it. It's the damnedest thing. He's a single-figure handi-capper, but he'll take a guy that's two or three strokes better and play him for so much money that the other guy dogs it and he doesn't. He plays above his ability if the money is high enough, where the normal reaction is to play worse when you play for more. For Doyle, a ten-thousand-dollar Nassau is like you and me going to the soda fountain." A Nassau is actually three bets for the agreed sum: front, back, and total. In a $10,000 Nassau, the player who wins the most holes in the first nine wins $10,000, the player who wins the most in the second nine wins $10,000, and the player who wins the most holes over all wins a further $10,000. "Most guys playing for that kind of money will dog it, but Doyle's got no fear. That guy's not afraid of anything."

An example: We were standing at the eighteenth green watching a match which at that point was even. The player farthest from the hole made a long, brilliant putt, and the ball rolled in. Brunson applauded with the rest. The other player's ball was only two feet from the flag; he had merely to tap it in to halve the hole. He squinted along the green, made one smooth practice shot, then hunched over the ball, concentrating fiercely. But at the point of impact he seemed to hesitate, and the ball rolled past the lip of the hole. There was a kind of massed sigh from the spectators; it seemed that they had all been holding their breath and then released it at the same moment. Brunson shrugged. "I lost eighty thousand betting on this game," he said equably. He added, "Let's go congratulate the loser. Everyone congratulates the winner."

"He's got a heart bigger than a watermelon," said the man from Albuquerque. "His generosity is unheard of in this cutthroat business. Maybe that's how he got to the top."

It was past noon, and the oil man and I were standing by Brunson's Lincoln Continental, waiting for a lift back to Binion's. Brunson himself was in the clubhouse settling up the morning's action. When he finally shambled out, he was smiling genially.

"How did it go?" asked the man from Albuquerque.

Brunson shrugged and said, "Win a few, lose a few." He opened the Lincoln's trunk, fumbled in a cardboard box, and passed around expensive pens with watches built into them and German hunting knives in leather sheaths. "Can you guys use these things?" he mumbled. When we started to thank him, he looked embarrassed and said, "I got this friend who owes me poker money, and he was kinda stuck. He gives these things to his salesmen, so I took some off him in part payment to help him out. It doesn't mean a thing."

He climbed into the car and yawned prodigiously. "I

didn't get but two hours' sleep last night," he said. "That never used to bother me none, but I guess I'm getting older. I reckon I'm going to have me a little siesta." He yawned again. "A little lunch, a little siesta."

We drove back in silence. But at four o'clock, when I went into the card room at the Horseshoe, Brunson was playing again. He was still there at midnight.

*　　*　　*

The evening after the Irish Republican Army hunger striker Bobby Sands starved himself to death in a Belfast prison, I shared a table in the Sombrero Room with a burly Texan. He was $28,000 behind, he told me, and had been playing nonstop for twenty-four hours. His sullen face was unshaven, and he was devouring a great mound of spareribs with his fingers. He ate ravenously, two-handed, and there was grease around his mouth, on the stubble of his chin, on his grimy T-shirt. He pointed a sparerib at the Las Vegas *Sun* lying beside his plate. "I cain't reckon it," he said. "A guy starving hisself to daith. It ain't nateral."

I said that it was inevitable — that the IRA wanted a martyr and Mrs. Thatcher was pigheaded.

"Waill," he said, eying me carefully, as though I had just made a large bet and he wanted to see if I was bluffing, "I reckon you coulda made yourself a millen dollars right here in this room taking bets on that. No one woulda credited it."

"There was no other way," I said.

"A cool millen," he answered longingly. "Easy as pie." Then he turned his attention back to the spareribs.

It was the only moment in my four weeks in Glitter Gulch when anyone referred to the outside world. A few days later, the news came that the Pope had been shot, but nobody mentioned it, despite the innumerable crucifixes dangling from the necks of both the players and the casino staff.

A man I know was playing in the three-dollar-and-six-dollar hold 'em game at the Golden Nugget on the night of Jimmy Carter's election to the presidency. In the small hours of the morning, he left the game briefly and went up to his room to get the results from TV. When he returned, he announced to the table at large, "We've got a new president — Jimmy Carter." The dealer stared at him coldly, as if he had broken some obscure house rule, and the man sitting next to him said, "The bet is three dollars." There was no other comment. Later that morning, the banner headline of the early edition of the Las Vegas *Review Journal* read "DEALERS LOSE TO IRS!" In the bottom right-hand corner was a small paragraph announcing, "Jimmy Carter New Pres."

After you have spent a period in Glitter Gulch, even the mountains off on the horizon no longer seem real; nor do the jet trails high above them. Everything is swallowed up by the fiction of action and a vast, insatiable narcissism. One afternoon, a tourist announced to the sunbathers around the pool at the Mint Hotel that a heavy loser had sat down in the lobby of Caesars Palace, put a gun in his mouth, and blown his head off.

"When?" asked the pool attendant.

"Yesterday," said the tourist.

A mousy-haired young woman who was resting between blackjack sessions looked up from her Harold Robbins novel and said, "*I* was at Caesars yesterday."

The professional gamblers inoculate themselves against this contagious unreality by betting on everything. Betting is the one sure way of engaging their attention. The more successful they are, the higher the bets must be. "I used to be able to play hard in all games, cheap and high," Brunson said. "But now I can only play high. I tell myself that's because there's no sense in wearing myself out for the big action, but the truth is I don't play well in small games, because the incentive is no longer there."

I asked what he meant by small.

"Well, two-hundred-and-four-hundred-dollar limit is small to me now, although at that level you can win ten or twenty thousand over a period of time," he said. "But we play so high out here — five hundred and a thousand, one thousand and two thousand, and no limit. In the games with the casino owners and the bookmakers and the dope dealers, there can be millions of dollars on the table. I guess I've got spoiled. As a player, I've got more experience now, but I don't have the desire and the concentration and the discipline unless the game is real high. When the stakes are big enough to catch my attention, then I revert to my old self. In fact, they make a joke about it. They say, 'Better not raise it up too high or Doyle will play better.' It's the same in everything — I wouldn't play golf unless I played for a lot of money, and I've *never* watched a football game or a basketball game without a bet on it. I'd go crazy with boredom." He added, "Not that I consider myself a compulsive gambler. I can go for long periods without making a bet, but if I do, I don't play golf, I don't watch ball games, I don't play cards. Man is a creature of his environment, and I guess I've just got used to it. When in Rome you gotta shoot Roman candles."

*   *   *

Brunson's inability to be interested in anything unless there is big money involved influenced him even when, in 1977, after he won the World Championship of Poker for the second year in succession, he took twelve months off from the tables to write a book about poker. He gathered a number of experts on games at which he felt himself not to be the final authority — Crazy Mike Caro on draw, Joey Hawthorne on lowball, Chip Reese on seven-card stud, David Sklansky on high-low split, Bobby Baldwin on limit hold 'em — and they talked into a tape recorder until he had accumulated mountains of transcripts. Then, Brunson, helped by a sportswriter named Allan Goldberg, organized these into a six-hundred-page book.

Like every serious poker player, Brunson had brooded at length on his wins and losses — especially his losses — analyzing hands and plays and players, refining his strategies over the years, learning from his own mistakes, and capitalizing on the mistakes of others. "But I'd never thought in a systematic way about what I was doing," he told me. "I knew I had a lot of ideas, but I had never clarified them precisely to myself. That year I spent writing the book was the hardest work I ever have done."

For the first edition, Brunson chose a peculiarly Vegas title: *How I Made Over $1,000,000 Playing Poker*. Later, he changed that to the less flamboyant *Super/System: A Course in Power Poker*. Like the titles, the prose will not win any prizes — except for its unwavering determination to split every infinitive. But as a postgraduate guide to the intricacies of high-level, high-stakes poker the work has no equal. The classic poker books, like Herbert O. Yardley's *The Education of a Poker Player*, concentrate on simple guidelines designed to disabuse beginners of the idea that poker is a gambling game and to instill in them the principles of conservative play. Brunson takes that kind of basic knowledge for granted, and also takes for granted the idea that everyone knows how to play tight. The strategies that interest him are those by which the experts outmaneuver each other when they are playing the finest of fine edges.

There are two types of poker books: the how-tos, which are more or less abstract and often contain a good deal of mathematics about probabilities and percentages, and the autobiographical, like Yardley's classic, in which examples and solid advice are sandwiched between racy stories about dramatic games. Recently, Johnny Moss, Amarillo Slim Preston, and Bobby Baldwin have cashed in on the fame brought them by their World Championships (Moss won in 1970, 1971, and 1974; Preston in 1972; and Baldwin in 1978) by writing — or having ghostwritten for them — maundering accounts of their lives and hard times, sometimes with, sometimes without practical advice from the horse's mouth. Brunson is both more modest and more ambitious. He is interested not in his image but in the endless intricacies of the game itself at the highest level. Yet, because he set out to think about how he and his colleagues play, the result is curiously personal, in places, for such a technical book. He writes:

> The very best players I know are extremely aggressive . . . And I firmly believe that's what accounts for the difference between a very good player and a truly top player. It's the dividing line. That's for sure.
>
> There's not a man alive that can keep beating on me. I refuse to let somebody keep taking my money

. . . and all the other truly top players are the same way. An aggressive player might do it for a while . . . keep leaning on me. But, at the first opportunity I get, I'm going to take a stand and put all my money in the pot.

It's like that little boy who keeps sticking his head up and keeps getting slapped all the time. Well, sooner or later he's *not* going to stick his head up any more. So if a guy keeps going on and on and keeps pounding on me . . . then me and him are fixing to play a pot.

The grammar may be shaky in places, the punctuation baroque, but the voice is distinct and the message is clear: aggression, constant aggression.

It is a strange contradiction of Brunson's imperturbable geniality away from the table, of his good humor, his generosity, and his sweet tooth. Johnny Moss looks exactly what he is: in Brunson's words, "a tough, tough cookie." Brunson, however, looks like a jovial creation of Chaucer's, overweight and liberal-handed, just as Jack Straus, another killer at the table, has all the charm and insouciance of Paul Newman in *The Sting*. I asked them if this double attitude didn't make life unduly complicated.

Brunson laughed, although without much enthusiasm. "You mean schizo — whatever it is?"

"No. Just complicated."

He nodded indulgently, as though humoring a small child. "When I sit down at the poker table, I'm there to win," he said. "Nothing complicated about that."

"Winning is everything," Straus said. "Doyle, when you played basketball back in college, did it bother you to lose? I had what they call a nervous stomach. I couldn't eat after we lost, and if any of my teammates were laughing and having a good time it really upset me. I couldn't sleep, either; I'd just lie there and think about the things I might have done. Poker's the same — it's all about competition. Different people are afraid of different things. Me, I'm afraid of embarrassment. If I lose, I don't give a damn about the money, but I just hate the embarrassment of being beaten."

Perhaps Brunson, Straus, and the other really high rollers can afford to be such easygoing company away from the table because while they are at the table, all their aggressions are expressed, accounted for, controlled. As Mickey Appleman said, admiringly and a little longingly, "Pettiness has no part in their lives."

The need to win and the need to be financially involved in anything that merits his attention stayed with Brunson when he came to publish his book. A number of publishing houses had approached him, but from his millionaire's perspective none of their offers made sense. "They offer you a peanut — five or ten percent — and then want to take all the rest," he told me. "I asked them to let me put up my share of whatever it cost to produce the book and make me a partner. They answered, 'We have the organization, the know-how, the sales force, the printers. You provide the text and you *are* a partner — for ten percent.' And they wouldn't shift, however much I argued. So finally I decided to go ahead and do it myself. Naturally, they told me it wasn't possible, but I answered, 'I've done everything I set out to do in my life. I reckon I'll do this, too.' So I got hold of a writer, and we set up a joint company, B. & G. Publishing — Brunson and Goldberg."

Never one to do things by halves, Brunson rented a lush suite of offices ("I looked like Doubleday"), hired a staff, installed a hundred-thousand-dollar computer, and, when the book was eventually published, with a price of a hundred dollars, advertised it in every paper in the country that had a circulation of more than a hundred thousand. But in the world beyond Las Vegas an excessively expensive book with a long-winded, unappealing title is hard to sell. And Goldberg, it turned out, knew less about marketing than Brunson had hoped. "I spent three hundred and fifty thousand dollars and had nothing to show for it except a book I was selling for a hundred dollars a copy," Brunson said. "People were buying it, but never on a profitable basis, and the overheads were eating me up. I planned to go ahead and publish other gaming books. I was really going to get into the book business. But I had it all wrong and the New York publishers got it right: I was into something I didn't know a damned thing about. Then Goldberg and I had a disagreement, so I bought him out and went ahead with a girl in charge. But she ripped me off, so now I do it all by myself. It's on a pretty small scale now, but at least it's making money."

B. & G. Publishing currently operates from a tiny office somewhere off the Strip. Brunson collects his mail from the post office and sorts it himself, carefully checking the order forms and the dates. His sole employee is a squat, smiling girl with sandy hair and a mouthful of metal. She hovered over him adoringly while he opened the morning's letters. "Take a look, honey," he said, brandishing an order slip with a check clipped to it. "This here is one of the forms we put out two years ago. Strange how things stick."

Brunson eventually sold out his first edition, of five thousand, then cut the price to a mere $50 and published a second edition, with the new, snappier title; that, too, is selling slowly but steadily. After all, the price is no more than an ante or an opening bet in what would be a rather small game for Brunson and his cronies. But he has had his action in publishing, and no longer has any illusions about beating the big houses at their own game. "It was like a toy," he said. "And I was just playing at being a businessman."

In his idle moments now, Brunson plays with the idea of running for Congress as an independent on a single-plank platform — a reform of the gambling laws that Robert F. Kennedy introduced in his effort to cripple the mob when he was attorney general. "They strike me as being unconstitutional, and a guy running in a gambling state like Nevada could maybe pick up a lot of votes," Brunson said. When I observed that it was hard to stay independent in a closed world like Washington, he shook his head serenely and said, "Everyone who goes into the political arena has political aspirations — most of them want to be president — so they are afraid to step on anybody's toes. It would be interesting to see what a guy could do if he didn't give a damn about his political career." He settled comfortably in his chair. "It's just a thought," he added.

Meanwhile, the book has worked against Brunson in his chosen career by making the competition more intense. "In the old days, if a guy came along and tried playing my aggressive game I would just move up a gear and play right back over him," Brunson told me. "But now they've read the book, they recognize what I'm doing, they think I'm bluffing, and call me. It's hampered my style. I used to be able to wreck a game without holding any cards at all, because I never got called. Now I need the cards."

The traditional strategy in no-limit hold 'em was to wait until you were dealt strong cards, like a big pair or an ace-king, and then lure as many people as you could into the pot with you by betting moderately at the start and moving in with a large bet after the flop. Brunson was the first to point out that these big hands could easily be broken when middling cards flopped, and that the hands of real value were small pairs or two small connected cards of one suit — a six and a seven of hearts, say — which an indifferent flop might turn into possible straights or flushes or threes of a kind. "They never used to play cards like that," he said. "When they raised, they always had big cards. So if you came in with small cards for a relatively small amount of money and beat those big hands, you would just break them. It was only a question of time until you did it. It was so easy it was like stealing. But now they've all read my book and they're smarter." He held up his hands, one a couple of inches above the other. "The difference between the top players and the good players used to be like this. The top players would let the inferior players round up the money; then they would beat them. The hometown champions would break their local games, then come out here and be broken by us. Now it's like this." He moved his hands together — one lying on the other. "It's getting harder all the time. Maybe that's not such a bad thing. At least, it's creating new players. Even so . . ." His head tilted quizzically, and he spread his hands as though in blessing. "If I had it to do again, I wouldn't write that book."

THE five weeks when the poker room at the Horseshoe is open are, for the professionals, what the weeks before Christmas are for Saks Fifth Avenue: the beginning or the end of their financial year, when they either make enough money to see them through to the next tournament or lose so much that they must hustle nonstop to survive the next eleven months. Yet financially the World Series itself matters to them a good deal less than the unofficial games. The tournament is a sideshow that brings in players from all over the country, and the professionals enter the big events mainly because honor and their devotion to the Binion clan dictate that they do so. But the official events are freeze-outs; everything depends on the players' getting the right cards at the right moment, since they cannot buy themselves back in after their chips are gone. In the side games, however, the money is virtually unlimited.

"I'd love to play in all the tournament events," Brunson said. "But there are so many good players entering that the overlay is too big; you can't figure to win them. So they are just going to consume your time and wear you out for the high-stakes side games. For instance, the first prize in the last event — the preliminary seven-card stud — is fifty thousand dollars. Now, I'm not averse to playing for three days and winning fifty grand, but that's just the first prize, and in that time I could be playing in a game where I could probably win that much. Not for sure — nothing's for sure in poker — but at least the money will be there, and I figure to win."

He figures to win: the top players gather from every state in the Union, and the Vegas professionals wait to be challenged by them, like knights in armor — or, rather, since this is the West, like the last of the gunslingers, loners in a dangerous profession. For them, the risk, challenge, and solitariness of their profession are a source of intense pride. Ask them about the lure of the way they live, and they talk about being free, outside the system, unanswerable to any boss; they tell you that they alone decide when they work and for how long; they boast that they cannot be put into any computer, though they then complain that the Internal Revenue Service treats them differently from other businessmen, taxing them on their winnings and making no allowance for their losses. They talk also, more vaguely, about the elation and release of "action," and take pride in their willingness to risk, if not their lives, at least their livelihoods when they think the odds are in their favor. Curtis Skinner, a Vegas regular known as Iron Man — because on the golf course he prefers not to use a wood — told me that in the 1950s Brunson played in a golf match when he had only $1500 to his name; he bet the whole sum on the front nine holes, lost, and was unable to play the back nine. "He'll gamble as high as his billfold will allow," Iron Man said. "And he'll bet it all on the first bet."

I had watched Iron Man playing poker, although never with Brunson, so I asked, "What about you?"

Iron Man is short and round-bellied, with a hooked and wrinkled Hogarthian face. He wears a green baseball cap and a track suit unzipped to show a large gold nugget dangling against his hairy chest from a golden chain. He shook his head and said, "I prefer the medium-sized games. I'm not trying to win a battleship."

The master of this absolute, all-or-nothing way of life is Jack Straus. In 1970, a terrible run at poker in Las Vegas reduced him to his last $40. Instead of quitting, he took the $40 to the blackjack table and bet it all on a single hand. He won, and continued to bet all the money in front of him until he had turned the $40 into $500. He took the $500 back to the poker game and ran it up to $4000, returned to the blackjack table and transformed the $4000 into $10,000. He finally bet the whole sum on the Kansas City Chiefs in the Super Bowl and won $20,000. In less than twenty-four hours, he went from near bankruptcy to relative affluence. The story is famous enough to have gone into gambling folklore, but the real point of it is his refusal to compromise. Each time he bet, he bet all the money he had, from the first $40 to the final $10,000.

It was a question of both pride and principle. In poker, one of the defining skills of a good player is money management — the ability to judge a bet and a situation subtly enough to make the maximum profit without being eliminated from the game. But Straus had had his back to the wall — $40 is not enough to sit down with even at a baby-stakes game — and when he sensed that his luck had turned he kept pressing. "The next best thing to gambling and winning is gambling and losing," said Nick the Greek Dandalos, who died broke on Christmas Day of 1966. He also said, "The exhilaration of this form of economic existence is beyond my power to describe." Straus himself, who, unlike the other professionals, reads books and travels outside America, prefers the proverb that Ernest Hemingway adopted as his own: "Better one day as a lion than a hundred years as a lamb." When Straus went big-game hunting in Africa, he had the paw of the first lion he shot mounted, with those words inscribed in gold around it. It was an act of self-definition as well as a tribute to the beast. "Some people play three hundred and sixty-five days a year in small games and try to grind out an existence," he said. "I just play in the very, very high games. There aren't that many of them, but I try to win enough to more than exist for the rest of the year."

In true gunslinger fashion, Straus prefers shorthanded games to ring games, involving eight or nine people, and is at his best with a single opponent — when aggression, initiative, and psychology are far more important than the cards. That is why he does not always do as well as he might in the World Series, where in the early stages patience is the most important virtue. But in 1981 he reached the final of the ace-to-the-five (no limit) lowball event, a particularly brutal version of draw poker in which certain conventionally strong hands — like threes of a kind and full houses — are worthless; aces count low, and the perfect, unbeatable hand is a small straight — ace, two, three, four, five — called "the wheel."

In the closing stages of the tournament, Straus was head-to-head with Mickey Perry, another Texan. The cards had been running in Perry's favor, and Straus seemed to be playing defensively, surrendering the antes with uncharacteristic docility whenever Perry bet. The television cameras moved in and out, the lights blazed, the crowd at the rail jostled and craned to see the action.

Finally, a big hand began to build. Perry bet $1000 after the deal, and Straus raised him $3000. There was a long pause. "When he thinks about it like that," Straus told me afterward, "I reckon he's drawing to a nine, maybe a good nine — two, three, four, nine, with some rubbish card." After great hesitation, Perry saw the three-thousand-dollar raise and drew one card, as though to demonstrate that Straus had read him accurately. Straus stood pat. The dealer dealt a card to Perry, who shuffled it into his hand and then, holding his cards almost flat against his chest, as though he were chronically nearsighted, squeezed them cautiously out into a fan. Again he checked. Without hesitation, Straus bet $27,000 — about three times the amount in the pot. There was another agonized pause, this one far longer than before. "Now I know what he's got," Straus told me. "He's made his nine, but it's rough. He's got a nine-eight." The crowd at the rail fell silent; even the television cameramen covering the event were still. Slowly, reluctantly, Perry separated $27,000 from the other chips in front of him: two and a half stacks of twenty five-hundred-dollar chips and four further five-hundreds — a squat gray mass like a crusader's castle. He waited, calculating how many chips that left him with, and waited again while he peered over at Straus's stacks to see how much he had remaining. Then, even more slowly and reluctantly, he pushed the $27,000 into the center and turned his cards over. They were exactly as Straus had reckoned: two, three, four, eight, nine. Straus tossed his cards face down into the discards, conceding the hand.

The television director moved forward immediately. "Mr. Straus," he asked, "for the sake of the viewing audience, may we see your cards?"

Straus had been, as usual, hunched in his seat, as if to conceal his enormous height. He uncoiled himself a little, reached for the cards, and turned them over slowly, one by one, his face as solemn as a hired mourner's at a wake: queen, queen, queen, jack, jack.

As one man, the railbirds burst into applause.

"Let's face it, gambling is a very romantic activity," said Jack Binion. "Movies reflect what people are looking for. Well, I wonder how many gamblers a big star like Clark Gable played in his career. We all daydream about people doing something we are a little bit afraid to do, and we make heroes out of those who pull it off. Jack Straus epitomizes that. He may not look suave, but he's independent, charming, cool in every situation, and he does things everyone kind of dreams about. There are a lot of guys out there who would love to be Jack Straus."

Straus himself takes pleasure in the freedom and the precariousness of the way he lives. Another Texas professional, Carl Canon, qualified as a lawyer before he decided to play poker for a living. "I chose the more honorable profession," he says. Straus, who was a basketball star at Texas A & M and has a degree in physical education, feels the same. "I have no regrets about my life," he says. "If I had it all to do again, I'd do it the same way."

As things are, Straus makes his experiences as a high roller the basis of endless outrageous stories, a new one for every occasion, each beginning, "Did I ever tell you about the time . . ."

The time when he was playing poker in the office of a used-car dealer. A customer came in just as the car dealer lost his sixth consecutive pot. "I'm interested in that red Chevrolet," said the customer. "Get the hell out of here," the dealer replied. "I don't have one car that will make it off the lot."

The time when the landlord walked in on a big game in a rented apartment. "I can't allow illegal gambling on my premises," he said. A wealthy businessman who was over $50,000 to the bad glared at him through the smoke and barked, "What's this place worth?" The landlord said, "I'd take thirty-eight thousand dollars for it." Without hesitating, the businessman wrote out a check and tossed it across the table. "Here's your thirty-eight thousand," he said. "Now get off my property."

The time when a stranger arrived in Houston wanting to play gin rummy for high stakes. "I told everybody to cut out the cussing and vulgarity, because this was a respectable businessman. (I always was a good judge of character.) So we played for a couple of days, and the game got higher and higher. Every time the stranger ran out of cash, he disappeared for a few minutes, then came back with another roll. About the tenth time he went out, I told the boys, 'Take it easy on him. This is one nice guy, and we don't want to spoil it, in case he feels like paying us another visit.' 'Jack,' said one of the players, 'it won't make no difference what he loses. I happened to see him out the window just now: he's got a suitcase full of money in the back of his car.' That was when I got to thinking that maybe he wasn't a legitimate businessman after all. A few days later, the FBI came around inquiring about him. It turned out he was a bank robber, Public Enemy Number One, wanted in every state from Tennessee to Texas. We ended up beating him out of all his money, but he was quite a gentleman about it. As he was leaving, I heard him say, 'Easy come, easy go.' "

The time, years ago, when his bankroll was far smaller than it is now and he owed money he didn't have to a high roller. "The guy said he was coming to collect on Monday, and I knew I couldn't raise the cash until Wednesday. But I daren't tell him that, or he would never trust me again. So while I was brooding about this problem, a buddy of mine walked in. When I told him what was wrong, he said, 'You think you're going bad? Look at this blue suit they've got me in. I started selling life insurance today.' Sure enough, he had on a blue suit, a white shirt, and a dark tie with stripes, his hair was cut short, and he was driving a black Ford instead of his fire-red convertible. That gave me an idea. I got hold of another kid with short hair — they were the only two clean-cut people I knew — and I gave them a couple of attaché cases and two billfolds with nothing inside. Then I got me a paper bag and stuffed it full of cut newspaper. I was supposed to meet the guy I owed money in front of the Hilton at noon. So my friends and I synchronized our watches and I told them to be waiting there in the Ford at eleven-fifty. Douglas, the guy I owed, was there at two minutes to twelve. Of course, he sees these guys in their suits and dark car, and he gets nervous. By the time I arrive, five minutes later, he's on tiptoe. As I round the corner, the two guys run up and grab me; they flash their wallets at me and shove me into their car. Douglas takes off running. By Wednesday, I had the money, so I called him on the phone. 'Don't say a word,' he said. 'I saw it all.' Then he hung up. It took me a week to get him paid."

One thread runs through all these stories: the sense of pleasure Straus derives from his chosen career. Unlike Johnny Moss or Doyle Brunson, Straus comes from a middle-class background, so money has never been a real problem for him. He began playing cards in high school — "I seemed to have the knack right from the start" — and at sixteen he won a car in a poker game. Since he did not yet know how to drive, he got the loser to park the car around the block from Straus's home and then had trouble explaining the acquisition to his parents. The family was close and religious; his parents disapproved of gambling and believed in duty. Straus's father managed a packing plant and lived his life strictly according to the conventions of the 1930s. "In those days, you were told you should work until you were sixty-five, then retire on two hundred a month," Straus said. "Well, my father, God bless his soul, worked very hard and did everything a person was supposed to do. But he died when he was fifty-eight, and never got to go anywhere or do anything." Straus took that lesson to heart and ordered his life according to two principles: to stay outside the system and to use his talents to enjoy life while he could.

Enjoyment matters more to him than profit. He once rented two rooms over a Chinese restaurant and opened a private card club. For anyone else, it would have been a license to print money, but not for Straus. "We were open two years, and all the profit from the place, plus fourteen thousand dollars more, went out in bad debts," he said. "Nobody ever went home broke. If you won, you got cash; if you lost, you got credit. But we played every day, and had a lot of fun. It was a financial disaster and a social success."

As the bank robber said, "Easy come, easy go," and Straus is a man to whom most things seem to have come easily: he is a superb athlete, a crack shot, a natural cardplayer. "Sports were my whole life until I was too old to play anymore; then gambling looked like the next-best thing," he said. "It was fun, it was action, it was a challenge." This accords with Jack Binion's theory that the top poker players are not only "mental athletes" but also former athletes, who turn to gambling when they no longer have the physical ability or the inclination for sport. "It's a question of excitement," Binion said. "Gambling is a manufactured thrill — you intensify the anticipation of an event by putting money on it. How long could a slot machine hold your interest if you didn't bet on it? Not very long. But once you insert your money the anticipation of the outcome becomes very important to you. You have manufactured a thrill between the time you make the bet and the time you get the result. When you were at school and were full of school spirit, there was high anticipation when you watched your school play a championship game. Then you get out of school, turn on the television, and watch Charleston play Houston at basketball. Neither team means anything to you, and maybe you don't even care that much about basketball, so your anticipation is not that high. But if you bet a hundred dollars on the result it will be 'Welcome back to that old school spirit.' In other words, gambling is a way of hyping an event."

But with time and custom it also becomes a habit of mind, even when the excitement needs no hyping at all. Straus once opened the door of his apartment to a friend who had gone berserk after a four-day alcoholic binge. The man charged in waving a gun, yelling that he was going to kill them all — Straus, his son, and a gambling friend. The drunk fired off one shot, wounding the gambler in the thigh, and then ordered all three of them to go down on their knees with their hands behind their heads. The boy and the wounded man did as they were told, but Straus remained standing, trying unsuccessfully to reason with the lunatic, and waiting for a chance to jump him. When the police arrived outside with guns and a bullhorn, the man became even more demented. "Where do you want me to shoot you?" he screamed at Straus. "In the stomach or between the eyes?" "I felt like saying, 'How about the big toe?' " said Straus. "But I was afraid he might not see the joke. It was the only time I was ever at a loss for words." Luckily for him, at that moment the police shouted from outside and the madman glanced at the window. Straus launched himself at him and knocked the gun from his hand. When it was all over, he asked the wounded gambler, "What did you make the price on me getting the gun before he killed me?" "I made you about eight-to-five dog," the friend replied. "Good Lord," said Straus. "I thought I was about even money. If I'd suspected I was an eight-to-five underdog, I wouldn't have had the nerve to jump."

It makes a good joke now, but at the time he was deadly serious. For the true gambler, there is a price for everything, even his own survival, and getting the right price adds an extra edge to the pure, addictive thrill of action. Nick the Greek ended his days playing five- and ten-dollar-limit draw in the poker parlors of Gardena, California, but when someone suggested to him that this was perhaps a comedown from his days of glory he replied haughtily, "It's action, isn't it?"

The other side of action is the competitive spirit, the intense desire to win against all comers and against all odds. "I wouldn't pay a ten-year-old kid a dime an hour to sit in a low-stakes game and wait for the nuts," Straus said. "If there's no risk in losing, there's no high in winning. I have only a limited amount of time on this earth, and I want to live every second of it. That's why I'm willing to play anyone in the world for any amount. It doesn't matter who they are. Once they have a hundred or two hundred thousand dollars' worth of chips in front of them, they all look the same. They all look like dragons to me, and I want to slay them."

From Straus's point of view, it makes perfect sense. To others, the only puzzle is that rich amateurs are willing to sit down and play with him and his colleagues, knowing that their chances of winning are so slim. When I asked Bobby Baldwin about this, he replied, "Poker is the only game in Las Vegas where you are competing against other people instead of against the house. If you beat the twenty-one table or the craps table, you get just so much satisfaction. But if you beat Jack or Doyle or me — well, that's the greatest thing in the world. Anyway, a lot of players who come out here can afford to lose — in fact, they probably write it off as entertainment. Sometimes they win, but even if they lose they can say, 'What the hell, at least I took a shot at those guys and gave it my best.' And they enjoy the game, they enjoy the company. We never have any arguments. Fortunes may change hands, but everyone is a perfect gentleman."

It sounded too good to be true, so I asked one of the amateurs who come out regularly for the World Series. Seymour Leibowitz is a sweet-natured, overweight fugitive from the garment trade and a destroyer of amateur games from Philadelphia to Miami. He does not, however, often win against the Vegas professionals. Why, then, beat his head against a stone wall? "This is the most fascinating group of men," he answered. "I've played cards all over the world, but nowhere is like this. These men are such good players and such good sports and so honorable that I just love it. As for the expense, if the money doesn't hurt a little there's no fun. I play within my means, but I play in the big games. I like them. That's my pleasure. I look on it as a month's vacation. If I took a trip around the world, it would cost me forty or fifty thousand dollars, because anything I do I like to do in style. Otherwise, what good is it? But at the end of a vacation you've got nothing. Whereas I come here and I go away with memories, pleasures, friends. It seems that the higher you play, the nicer the men."

In 1981, at the annual prize giving that ends the World Series of Poker, Seymour Leibowitz was given a special award for being "the most congenial player in the tournament."

9

FOR the talented, Jack Binion is fond of saying, Las Vegas is the land of milk and honey, and for the rest it is a burial ground. Perhaps that is one way of explaining the prodigious crime rate, which the local papers find harder to disguise than to report. All the losers in the world come to Vegas in the hope of changing their luck, but losers are losers wherever they go, and eventually they become desperate. Hence the muggings, the violence, the theft.

Hence, too, the depression. When the regulars in the low-limit games are doing well, they earn pocket money and try to persuade themselves that they are making a living. Most of them are good enough to know the probabilities of filling a hand and to calculate automatically the odds offered by every pot. And because the ante is small they can sit for hour after hour waiting for bombproof cards. This gives them a tremendous advantage over impatient visiting tourists. But it is not enough to beat the house rake — the few dollars taken by the casino from every pot, which chips away like a stonemason at winners and losers alike.

Every so often, one of the regulars has a miracle night when everything goes right for him. But then he has to fight the temptation to take his winnings to the bigger game at the next table. At the Golden Nugget, the difference between the three- and six-dollar-limit hold 'em game and the ten- and twenty-dollar is a quantum leap in skill as well as in money. Some regulars make the move, filled with unreasoning confidence; most are back the next night at the smaller game, broke again and scratching around to survive.

In the meantime, the physical strain eats away at them as remorselessly as the house rake. Their backs ache from their slouching in chairs, their arms ache from their leaning them against the raised leather edge of the table, their skin is soggy and unaired from their playing all night and sleeping all day, their paunches sag, their eyes are muddy, their digestion is ruined by countless cups of coffee and starchy, irregular meals gobbled hastily in the half hours they are allowed to be away from the table and retain their seats.

As for conversation, the only talk is in the short breaks while the dealer fans a fresh deck of cards across the baize, checks them, and shuffles.

"How are things back in Utah?" asked a weathered, elderly man.

"Wet when I left," said his weathered, elderly neighbor. "How's the back?"

"Better since I quit the truckin' business."

"Your bet," said the dealer to the first elderly man.

Mickey Appleman remarked to me that a lot of people don't fit in where they are, but Las Vegas takes anybody. More important, I realized, it never comments. One evening, a tall, dignified woman in her early seventies, who looked like the late Queen Mary, sat down at the small hold 'em game. Her face was refined, with small features made delicate by age; her dress was a sedate black and white; her silver hair was piled in a discreet beehive. She smiled politely whenever she raised, and when she won she said "Thank you" to the dealer as he pushed the chips toward her. Every inch a lady except for one detail: pinned to the front of her beehive with a wooden toothpick was a neatly folded paper towel to shield her eyes from the glare. Nobody seemed to notice.

Nor did anyone comment on the man, solemnly eating his way through the buffet in the Sombrero Room, who was so obese that his tiny, bald head seemed to belong to another body entirely; he looked as if he were trapped in an overinflated balloon. He peered about from the center of his great mass like a tortoise, horn-rimmed spectacles at the end of his little nose, his eyes protuberant and astonished.

There were times at the beginning of my stay when Las Vegas seemed more like a raree show than like a vacation city. But after a while I, too, no longer noticed.

*　　*　　*

One afternoon, I shared a lunch table in the Sombrero Room with one of Binion's dealers. He was a skeleton-thin young man with large, hurt eyes behind large, thick glasses. His name, according to the plastic tag on his shirt, was Ronnie. There was a book beside him on the padded bench, and on the table were a loose-leaf file and a calculator. When I sat down, he was shuffling through the papers and punching figures into the calculator with a speed and dexterity that seemed inappropriate to the hurt look in his eyes.

He nodded contentedly at my press badge, but when I asked him which game he had been dealing he answered vaguely and seemed disappointed. He closed his file and watched me patiently while I ate, and then, when I filled my pipe, he pulled out a cigarette and waited for me to light it for him. Finally, he said, "I guess you don't know who I am." I looked at his name tag again and said, "Ronnie." His eyes deepened behind the thick lenses, and he smiled diffidently. "Used to be Suzie," he said. He riffled through the file and extracted an old clipping. The headline said, "Sex Change Dealer Returns to Binion's Horseshoe." He told me he had been in the navy — in the Caribbean during the Cuban missile crisis — but when he got out nothing went right. Between 1970 and 1976, he made thirty-six attempts to kill himself with sleeping pills, but in the hospitals nobody seemed to understand — not even the psychiatrists. In 1970, he had had a sex-change operation in New Jersey. Later, as Suzie, he came out to Las Vegas and became a dealer. "I did all right," he said. "But somehow it didn't solve the problem."

"Which problem?" I asked.

His huge eyes fixed me, unblinking. "Loneliness," he said.

Not until 1980 did he find someone willing to listen to

him. The man was an evangelist, and through him Suzie found God, was born again, and proved it by having another sex change, back to Ronnie. "It was nothing," he said. "I had a mastectomy and I cut my hair. It wasn't painful — not like the first operation." I asked if it had made him happier, and he nodded. "I used to be terrified of dying and of growing older. In that order. Now I know there isn't going to be any death. The day you die is the first day of your life." He waited for me to comment, and when I didn't he nodded at my press tag and said, "Reading helped me. I read Dale Carnegie's *How to Win Friends and Influence People*, and it changed my life. A great book." When I asked him what else he had read, he patted the large book on the bench beside him and said, "The Bible. There's more truth and wisdom in this than in any other book in the world." Then, suddenly, briefly, he was off, talking about peace and calm and contentment in the vague, singsong voice of a child repeating a lesson learned by rote. His eyes unfocused, and for a moment he seemed lonelier than anyone I had ever met — as though loneliness were the element he moved in, like a fish in water.

A group of players wandered in and settled at the next table. Ronnie blinked, shook his head, eyed them uneasily. He finished his recitation, but without conviction, and began to fiddle with his calculator. When the conversation finally turned to poker, as all conversations in the Sombrero Room eventually did during the tournament, he rattled off odds and probabilities like any other Vegas regular. It was only when I got up to leave that he remembered that his bizarre sexual sideshow had made him a Vegas celebrity. "There's a big article about me coming up in the *National Enquirer*," he said. "Be sure to read it."

"Of course," I said. But later, whenever I saw him, he pretended not to recognize me, as though he felt he had betrayed himself.

*   *   *

The freak shows were easier to take from a distance, and the view from my twelfth-floor window at the Golden Nugget — across the back lots, the railroad tracks, and the desert to the ring of blue mountains — was always soothing. One morning, I was awakened by the sound of a band, faint but distinct through the double glazing. Down below, diminished and foreshortened by the drop, a convention of Shriners was parading along the cross street: garishly uniformed brass bands, men in flowing Turkish robes and fezzes, clowns, floats, more bands, a pack of jokers in mobile beds, grown men driving miniature cars. Two vans were parked around the corner, directly below me, dispensing cans of cold beer. The parade broke up abruptly when it reached them, then re-formed haphazardly, drinking as it went. Balloons whirled about in the hot wind, rose, drifted off toward the railroad tracks. A squad of comic motorbikes wobbled past, a fire engine with a waving, motley crew, then more grown men in toy cars. At the rear of the parade was a shabby, ramshackle group of stragglers ambling along after two equally shabby, ramshackle camels. They were led by a man carrying a banner embroidered with "Whittier Shriners." That evening, the downtown casinos were full of Shriners who had discarded their fancy dress and were pumping away at the slots and whooping it up at the craps tables. Unlike Whittier's favorite son, Richard Nixon, none of them played poker.

As the days passed, I spent a good deal of time at the

bedroom window, watching for a change in the relentlessly good weather. At dusk, the haze cleared and the sunset came rose-pink beyond the folded mountains. One evening, a sliver of new moon poised above them, briefly upstaging the moving glitter of the town below. But by then I was sufficiently under the spell of the place to wonder if seeing the new moon through glass boded bad luck.

* * *

One afternoon, I walked the dozen and a half blocks to the Gambler's Book Club, which is in a working-class residential area just off Charleston Boulevard, between downtown and the Strip. Within a few blocks of the hotel — past the bus station and the Nevada National Bank, with its sign offering DRIVE-IN TV BANKING — the sidewalks gave out, the tourists disappeared. The houses were one-story and makeshift, like encampments of industrial nomads, with elderly, battered cars parked in front of them. But each was set in its own little garden, shaded by palm trees or tatty cottonwoods or bougainvillea, and the wide streets were miraculously quiet after the din of Glitter Gulch. Birds chirped from the trees, children played on the parched grass, and there were dogs sleeping in the shade under the porches. In four weeks in Clark County, these were the only pets I saw, apart from two Seeing Eye dogs waiting patiently while their blind owners primed the slots at the Mint.

The Gambler's Book Club has a gigantic triangular sign suspended point downward over its entrance but is otherwise unlike anything else in Las Vegas. It is a bookshop, a publishing house, a print shop, a mail-order service, and also a club where gamblers, theorists, writers, researchers, journalists, and kibitzers — most of them visitors — drop in to browse and chat and find out who else is in town. The bookshop proper, which used to be a pizza parlor, is a restful, rather scholarly room with over a thousand titles on the shelves — from thrillers to mathematical treatises, all of them on gambling. Behind the shop, in what used to be the rambling premises of an Italian food company, are offices, storerooms, rooms where books are bound and packed, and all the smooth gadgetry of modern business: electronic typesetting machines and computers for handling the inventory and the mail-order lists. The rare books — including six autographed by Edmond (According to) Hoyle himself, the only begetter of gambling rules — are kept in what was once a meat freezer.

The proprietors of this extraordinary specialist enterprise are John and Edna Luckman. On the principle that people live out their names (the manager of an English West Country crematorium is a Mr. Ash), Luckman began his career as a bookmaker in Santa Monica, then came to Las Vegas, where he worked in the casinos for twelve years, starting as a blackjack dealer and eventually becoming a pit boss at the Tropicana. But gambling interested him more as a subject than as a way of life. He was fascinated by old books on gaming — his collection is now in the library of the University of Nevada — and he turned to printing when a Las Vegas church elder parked a printing press in his carport. Luckman is also a do-it-yourself enthusiast, happiest when he has a screwdriver in his hand, and the machine fascinated him. He tried printing his own stationery, then bought better equipment and decided to reprint some of his gambling books that were no longer in copyright. He started with

The Racing Maxims of "Pittsburgh Phil," written by a legendary horse bettor, and branched out into a series of "Facts" books — *Facts of Blackjack, of Craps, of Keno, of Roulette, of Slots* — which were simple paperback guides to help the Vegas punters. The "Facts" books have now sold well over two million copies, and Luckman's mom-and-pop store has an annual turnover of more than half a million dollars. It also has a mailing list of customers from Indonesia to Poland. The list is particularly strong on inmates of state prisons. The wardens of federal penitentiaries do not allow Luckman's publications in their institutions. He approves of their decision — "I think they should stock up on law books" — but disapproves of the manager of a local casino who has refused to sell his books because they advise moderation.

The advice is typical of the man and the whole enterprise. Luckman, who held a recent American Booksellers Association conference spellbound with a demonstration of the three-card monte trick, gambles hardly at all and only for very small sums. His assistant, Howard Schwartz, who edits the club's magazines, *Casino & Sports* and *Systems & Methods*, is a thin, diffident, academic young man who used to be a schoolteacher in Colorado and calls himself "a frightened, conservative bettor." Both of them have the obsessed enthusiasm of the scholar for his special subject, and both are slightly contemptuous of the fact that so few of their customers are locals. "I bet we don't have six dealers who come here on a regular basis," Luckman says. "Players aren't readers." He seems to believe that anyone who gambles merely for the money or the thrill of action is somehow missing the subtlety of the enterprise. He is a bluff, friendly man with a drooping face and thick horn-rimmed glasses, but his attitude toward his clients is philosophical, resigned, like that of a social worker toward a street gang.

Several of his authors are academics fascinated by the mathematics of gambling or, at a lower level, adept at offering deanlike advice to casino freshmen. Very few are professional gamblers, who, according to Mickey Appleman, are usually "unsuccessful, talented people, highly intelligent but unable to fit in with the straight world." An exception is David Sklansky, who makes his living at the poker tables and has written three books for Luckman, including an ambitious treatise called *Sklansky on Poker Theory*. In other ways, however, he fits Appleman's definition precisely. The son of a professor of mathematics, he grew up in Teaneck, New Jersey, and attended the University of Pennsylvania. "Not Penn State," he insists, "the University of Pennsylvania. There's a major difference: the University of Pennsylvania is part of the Ivy League." It is not a distinction likely to impress his gambling colleagues, but it matters to him, even though he dropped out after a couple of years. "I didn't like taking courses I wasn't interested in," he said. "I didn't want to go through all that rigmarole." Since he had inherited his father's mathematical ability, he took a job as an actuary, but that, too, did not last. "One day, I came up with a new technique for solving a problem — a shortcut that made it a third less time-consuming. When I explained it to my boss, all he said was 'If you want to do it that way, it's O.K. by me.' He refused to pass the idea on to anyone else. In other words, I knew something no one else knew, but I got no recognition for it." In appearance, Sklansky is like one of Dostoevski's intolerant student revolutionaries: broad face, trimmed beard, steel spectacles, styleless clothes. His voice is careful but faintly obsessed. "In poker, if you're better than anyone else you make immediate money," he says. "If there's something I know about the game that the other person doesn't, and if he's not willing to learn or can't understand, then" — his voice rises, emphasizing each word — "*I take his money.* By rights, that guy who ran the actuarial office should have been broke; he shouldn't have been my boss. But in the business world things aren't like that. I was always being told what to do by incompetent people, and I hated it. The world is full of idiots, and I can't handle it. I can't handle the politics involved. But this town gives me what I want. I like the freedom of the gambler's life, I like being my own boss, I like the way you are rewarded directly according to your ability, not according to what people think of you."

Still, Sklansky is in some respects an odd man out among the Vegas professionals. The top players take pride in the times they have gone broke and bounced back; their overriding ambition is to beat their peers, not the suckers. In contrast, Sklansky has never been broke, and does not intend to start now. His attitude is encapsulated in the first chapter of *Poker Theory*, which is called "Getting Off on the Right Foot." It begins, "When we play, we must realize, before anything else, that we are *out to make money.*" The italics are his, and they are typical of the dour, businessman's fervor with which he approaches the game. Perhaps a comfortable childhood in Teaneck, New Jersey, is not the best preparation for a lifetime's commitment to anything as marginal or disreputable as poker.

I asked Sklansky what his parents thought of his profession.

"Initially, they disapproved," he said. "But then not so very many people have three titles to their name in the big catalogue *Books in Print*. After they saw that, they began to feel a little different about what I do. And I make good money; that always makes parents proud. It's obvious to them now that I'm not a degenerate gambler. In fact, there are people in this town who say I don't have any gamble in me at all. I don't consider that an insult. On the contrary, I think of myself as a game player, not a gambler. When I was at school, I was very good at mathematical aptitude; on the standardized tests I usually got perfect scores. But my best subject was probability, which depends less on mathematics than on ingenuity and the ability to think. It is that ability which I have applied to poker. In my book on theory, I stress logic above everything else. Whenever I lose a pot, I sit for a minute and work out what I did wrong and how I could have done better. The champion players have an incredible natural instinct for the game. I don't have that instinct, but I try to make up for it by study and thinking. What took them ten years of experience I can work out in an hour with a pencil and paper. I'm like someone who has studied the biomechanics of golf and never makes technical errors, while they are like people with such huge talent for the game that their mistakes don't matter. But sometimes they come to me with complicated problems, for technical advice, just as Jack Nicklaus would go to his coach, even though he can beat him."

By any normal standards, of course, Sklansky is an exceptionally good player, with endless powers of concentration. "Everything that happens at the table has meaning," he says, and he is able to think out logically the implications of each small sign in each new deal.

But that huge natural talent the champions possess is a question of imagination rather than logic, and it enables them to take cards that Sklansky would never consider playing and turn them into winning hands. For example, in a game of no-limit hold 'em Jack Straus was dealt the worst two cards in the pack, a seven and a deuce of different suits. But he was "on a rush," so he raised anyway, and only one other player stayed with him. The flop was dealt: seven, three, three, giving Straus two pairs — sevens and threes. He bet again, but as he did so he saw his opponent's hand reach quickly for his chips, and he knew he had made a mistake. The man, he realized, had a big pair in the hole; with great confidence, he raised Straus $5000. At that point, the logical move was to fold, since Straus was certain he was beaten and only a bluff could save him. But he called, thereby sowing doubt in the other player's mind. The dealer turned over the fourth card: a deuce. It paired Straus's second hole card but did not improve his hand, since there was already a communal pair of threes on the table. Without hesitating, Straus bet $18,000. There was a long, long silence while the other man considered the implications of the bet. Then Straus leaned forward, smiling his most charming, lopsided smile. "I'll tell you what," he said. "You give me one of those little old twenty-five-dollar chips of yours and you can see either one of my cards, whichever you choose." Another silence. Finally, the man tossed over a yellow-and-green chip and pointed to one of the cards face down in front of Straus. Straus turned it over: a deuce. Another long silence. The only logical explanation for Straus's offer was that the two cards in front of him were the same, so the flop gave him a full house with three deuces. The other man folded his winning hand.

"It's just a matter of simple psychology," Straus said later.

In poker, as in everything else, imagination starts where logic falters, and transforms reality for its own ends, as Straus did with his unplayable cards. His move was not just a bluff; it was play in the truest sense — a kind of wit, both stylish and elegant. "Everybody has a romance with life," Mickey Appleman said. "But most people relinquish it as they grow up and settle down with a job and a family. There are some people, though, who never give it up; they hold on to that portion of their childhood. For them, gambling is a replacement of the fantasies they had as children. I guess I'm like that. For me, the fantasy in gambling is not monetary. It's a question of fulfillment: being who I really am, doing things well, being involved — just feeling good."

Appleman's background is very much like Sklansky's, and in terms of poker ability there is probably not much difference between them. But Appleman became a gambler after a long period of confusion and self-questioning, because gambling solved problems he had previously been unable to cope with, and, by some absurd psychological sleight of hand, was far more emotionally rewarding than his previous career — work with the deprived and the addicted, for which he had thrown over the promise of the lucrative career his M.B.A. had qualified him for. Sklansky, on the other hand, is haunted by "the straight world" and sees poker as, he said, "a stepping stone" to something else. "The ability to analyze gambling situations is a microcosm of more important things," he told me. "Almost anything can be put into a mathematical model, although most people don't know that. I'm able to take nonmathematical situations and analyze them using logical techniques. Eventually, I would hope that the fact that I've written books and am therefore well known would enable me to branch into other fields. Perhaps some company will think, David Sklansky has the ability to look at situations and see logically what's supposed to be done, so maybe he's worth taking a shot at. We don't need him to start as a clerk; we'll let him skip fourteen steps and make him vice president in charge of systems analysis."

It seems a strangely inappropriate ambition for a man who has settled in the fantasy capital of the world and makes a living from the persistent logical exploitation of other people's weaknesses. But, as John Luckman said, "players aren't readers." So perhaps the few who, like Sklansky, not only read but also write about what they are doing are so out of the usual Vegas run that they develop a disproportionate belief in the power of the printed word. Luckman himself, despite his turnover and his mailing list, has no such illusions.

10

For the westbound wagon trains, the Nevada desert was a barrier, a destructive element to be suffered and endured. Now, thanks to air conditioning, it is the state's main attraction. Elsewhere in the United States that May, there were cold snaps and sudden thaws; there were tornado warnings in Alabama and hurricanes in Florida. But in Las Vegas the weather was a steady state, as in a controlled experiment. The sun shone, the desert wind blew, the illuminated thermometer at the top of the Mint registered eighty-five to ninety-five degrees day after day.

Then, on the morning of May 15, a minor miracle occurred. When I got out of bed and went to the window, the sun was gone. Beyond the parking lots, the pawnshops, and the railroad tracks, the mountains were shrouded in dark veils, which were vaguely wavering at the edges and moving slowly toward the town. By noon, there was rain. The air was cool, and the rackety streets of Glitter Gulch were pervaded by the faint, musky scent of dust finally laid. Later that afternoon, the little pool at the Mint was empty, fresh, delectable. The following day, it was closed. The air temperature had dropped to a mere seventy-three degrees, which by Vegas's standards is too cold for swimming.

But when the main, and final, event of the 1981 World Series of Poker began, three days later, the heat had clamped down again. Despite the air conditioning, Binion's Horseshoe was sweltering, although the contestants did not seem to notice. Set apart from the journalists, the television crews, and the spectators, who had been packed against the rails since early morning, were seventy-five poker players — two more than the previous year — who had put up $10,000 apiece for the privilege of playing no-limit hold 'em for the title of World Champion.

"That's American democracy," a journalist from New York said. "It costs ten Gs to enter, but anyone who's got that kind of money to spare can sit down and take his chances with the best players in the world."

I had the impression that if he could have written it off against expenses he would have sat down himself. And that is what distinguishes the poker tournament from other sporting events. When Norman Mailer went to Kinshasa in 1974 to cover the Ali-Foreman fight, he may have gone on a training run with Ali, but not even Mailer, who prides himself on his boxing and still works out regularly, would ever have dreamed of going into the ring with the man. In the looming presence of Ali or Foreman, there are limits to the illusions one can have about one's physique and athletic prowess. Not so in poker. The seventy-five entrants in the big event are all mental athletes of exceptional ability, the fine tip of a pyramid of well over fifty million players. But they are not much to look at: mostly middle-aged and overweight, with sallow, pouchy faces, bloodshot eyes, nicotine-stained fingers, five-o'clock shadow.

Stu Ungar, the defending champion, is in his middle twenties but looks like a scrawny teen-ager, loose-jointed and deathly pale, with a nervous, rapid-fire, slurring voice and a slightly simian jaw — "a dead ringer," said Jack Straus, who is fond of him, "for Vera, the doctor in the *Planet of the Apes*." Johnny Moss and Puggy Pearson never progressed beyond the third grade at school, and another top player, I was told, can barely read or write. Yet all of them know the precise percentages offered by every pot; at any point of the deal they can tell you which cards have already fallen, how many are left in the pack, how many will help them, and the exact odds on their making a hand. They know all this with complete accuracy, but instinctively, through card sense, experience, and innate mathematical ability. Even those who have gone through school often adopt an innocent, aw-shucks, country-boy air to confuse the opposition. That, too, is poker.

So the bright, educated outsider can persuade himself that he is in with a chance, particularly since there is an element of luck in any card game. Chess is a game of pure information — like poker with all the cards exposed — where the better player will always win; that is why a computer can be programmed to play it so well. But the only way a computer could be made to play top-level poker would be by introducing a randomizing factor into the program which would correspond both to the element of bluff and to the random way the cards fall. When the cards are particularly kind, even a sucker can beat a really good player. But not for long. That is why the poker tables at Las Vegas are called "the graveyards of hometown champs." Poker players who have beaten their local games in all corners of the United States come to Vegas to test their skills, like tennis players converging on Wimbledon. Nearly all of them go home broke.

*   *   *

At midday on Monday, May 18, 1981, seventy-five of the most spectacular survivors in the poker world were milling nervously around the Sombrero Room. Less than a quarter of them had any real hope of walking away with the title, but even those elect few were strung up like racehorses. They seemed to have difficulty staying still. They moved about from group to group, from table to table, chatting briefly and then moving on, hovering, listening to the gossip, getting another perspective, sizing up the opposition, charging themselves up on the excitement.

Even Doyle Brunson seemed nervous, although his large, comforting presence translated tension into a faint, subliminal gloom. "The only way you can approach it is to think it's just another poker game," he said. He shifted uneasily in his chair, like an iceberg settling in the water. "That's not strictly true, of course. Today is the biggest day of the year for poker players. And every year it gets bigger. Seventy-five contestants means three-quarters of a million prize money. Three hundred seventy-five thousand dollars for the winner. Whichever way you reckon it, that's a good payday."

The local bookmakers had made him the favorite to win the title for the third time — the previous year Stu Ungar had beaten him in the final — but that was an added burden, and he did not want it. When I mentioned it, he shook his head doubtfully and said, "I'm not playing as well as last year." The iceberg settled further in the water. "But I'll play hard and maybe something will happen. You have to get a lot of breaks to come through that many players. In a freeze-out, when you can't reach back and take more chips, the best player won't necessarily win. There's a lot of luck involved. I guess that's what attracts so many players. You have to have the right cards at the right time in order to get down to the last table. Once you're there, then the best player has a good chance. The most important money is your first ten thousand. If you can get your chips up to twenty thousand, where you can lose a pot without crippling yourself, then you're in with a chance. But if I lose the first couple of pots I play, there is not much I can do about it; the next one I put money in I've got to win. That makes you push your hands a little bit when you start getting low on chips. I never was much of a short-stack player. I like to have a lot of money in front of me. If another guy has more, it affects my style of play. Some of the others aren't like that — they just sit there and wait and try to catch a hand and double up. I like to chop around and win small pots and gradually build up my stack. Then if a big pot comes I play it. But the main thing about tournaments is to try to win small pots early, then hope to catch a break or two. Everybody at the last table will have had his share of luck."

I asked him what he meant by not playing well, since he had been winning steadily in the side games, and Brunson, even when slightly off form, is better than almost any other player.

"The first time I won the tournament, I got lucky in a couple of key pots: I had the worst hand going in but managed to outdraw the guy each time when all my chips were in the center. But the second time I won the title I didn't make a single mistake the whole three days. I never jeopardized my stack unnecessarily, I read my opponents right every time, I threw away strong hands when I sensed I was beaten, and my chips never went down; they just built and built all the way. This year . . ." He shrugged. The iceberg quaked slightly. "I dunno. If I can get some soft spots to start with, so I can build up my stack . . ." He rose majestically to his feet. "I'm going to go supervise the draw and make sure they don't stick me at the same table as Johnny Moss, Bobby Baldwin, Puggy Pearson, and Jack Straus, the way they do every year."

* * *

Jack Straus was complaining about the prize money. "I don't reckon it should be divided up — half to the winner, twenty percent to the runner-up, and so on," he said. "Nine people — the whole last table — are going to walk away with cash. That's not what a competition is about. The winner should take the whole seven-fifty."

Today, even Straus seemed to be on edge. He shifted from foot to foot, like a horse sensing bad weather, and peered about, from his enormous height, over the crowded heads. A slim, straight-backed young woman in a mauve jump suit was hesitating at the entrance to the

Sombrero Room. Straus signaled to her — half wave, half salute. She waved back and threaded her way through the crowd to join him.

Most of the women poker players have lacquered hair and tired faces, which make even the young ones look middle-aged. Betty Carey, however, is in her midtwenties and looks younger. She has what used to be called "an outdoor-girl complexion," a narrow, Cupid's-bow upper lip, a disarming smile, and eyes like curiously carved ice: the upper lids straight, all the curve in the lower half. Her profile is slightly aquiline, like Samuel Beckett's, but is offset by a discreet mass of curls. A Renaissance face, the kind that Piero della Francesca painted in profile — not the kind of face common in Vegas. Yet she is also one of the most formidable poker players in the country, savagely competitive. Not only was she entered in the tournament, but in the side games before the tournament's big event she was sitting down with the fiercest of the tigers — Brunson, Moss, Baldwin, Pearson — and taking their money night after night. Then Straus stopped her in her tracks.

My first sight of her had been at the beginning of that game: a demure and perilously young woman sitting across the table from six professional poker champions, like Chris Evert Lloyd taking on Borg, McEnroe, and Connors. She was very much at her ease, sipping wine, smiling at them over a mountain of black and gray chips so large that she was barely able to encircle it with her arms. Above them, her delicate, quattrocento head and shoulders seemed oddly out of proportion, as though the chips were some late, strange pregnancy. That was at eight o'clock, and she was winning well over $200,000. When the game ended, eight hours later, she was broke;

thirty thousand had gone to Brunson, most of the rest to Straus when his full house beat her three eights.

Not long before, Straus had given her an ivory pendant as a present — an eighteenth-century Chinese gambling chip inscribed with two words, *Love* and *Dread*. He had said, "It means you're going to love playing with those suckers, Betty, but you're going to dread playing with me." Now the prophecy had been fulfilled.

"You watch," Straus muttered as she joined us. "She's the only person who thinks the way I do." He touched her arm and smiled amiably down at her. "Betty," he said, "how do you reckon the prize money should be divided?"

She did not hesitate: "Winner take all."

"I told you so," Straus said triumphantly.

She smiled at him, and then glanced vaguely around the packed room. "Full house," she said.

"Here's hoping," Straus said.

The conversation languished.

Betty Carey is from Wyoming, and her mother still lives there. Her father was a war veteran, badly wounded in one leg, and the Wyoming cold was bad for his circulation. So during the winters he moved down to Las Vegas, where he set up as an importer of seafood for some of the downtown restaurants. Eleven years ago, when Betty was in her teens, he was killed in a road accident out in the Clark County desert.

"Blowout?" I asked when I first met her, with Straus.

"Murdered." She spoke the word with no particular emphasis, as though it were "coronary" or "cancer." His car, she explained, had been forced off the road three times. Twice, he had managed to fight it back onto the pavement; the third time, it had overturned, killing him.

I asked what had happened to the other driver. "He disappeared," she said laconically. "Case unsolved." But the episode gave her, at least, the measure of male aggression. Four years ago, she graduated to high-stakes poker, and since then, Straus said, she has become "boss gambler down there in Houston," where she now lives. Boss gambler also in Vegas until she found herself head to head with the charming but relentless Jack Straus. After that disaster, she disappeared from the Horseshoe for a few days, presumably to raise the cash to pay her debts. The evening she returned, she was standing with him in the Sombrero Room when a gambler to whom Straus owed money came up. Straus pulled out a gigantic wad of bills and began counting them out.

Betty smiled at him. "I just bet that's money you got from some po' li'l gal," she said.

"Sure is." Straus returned the roll to his back trouser pocket. "And I keep it right here, honey, next to my heart."

Now they were standing with Straus's teen-age son — a beardless double of his father, equally tall — and Straus's gofer, Larry Morrell, who looks uncannily like the old movie comic Jerry Colonna: bald as a billiard ball, big black mustache, and an apparently unlimited supply of enthusiasm for everything. But on this occasion even Larry seemed to have run out of things to say.

"What's the time?" Straus asked fretfully.

Most of the Vegas gamblers are festooned with jewelry: gold rings stuck with outsize diamonds, heavy gold chains and bracelets, some with their names studded on them in diamonds, and every variant of the world's most expensive wrist watches. Even Doyle Brunson, who is not otherwise given to ostentation, wears an Audemars-Piguet with diamond numerals and a platinum chain bracelet. But Straus wears no ornaments at all. "When I was a kid, I wanted a five-dollar watch, then a ten-dollar watch, then a hundred-dollar watch," he said. "When I made money, I wanted a Rolex, then a Patek-Philippe. Now I realize that the real luxury is not to know the time." But in the few minutes before the world hold 'em championship began he seemed to be regretting that luxury.

"Ten of one," Betty Carey said.

"Let's go," Straus said.

*   *   *

For weeks, the poker players had been dressed as though for a back-room game in a Texas pool hall: jeans and soiled T-shirts or cheap cotton plaid cowboy shirts from South Korea with imitation-mother-of-pearl buttons. Now the poker room was like a fashion parade. Perhaps the presence of the television cameras had inspired the change, or perhaps it was the arrival, two nights before, of Crandall Addington, a millionaire in oil and Texas real estate, who is an amateur, and who invariably sets the standard of elegance at the Horseshoe. Addington once played for five consecutive days and nights without loosening his Dior tie. Last year, he appeared in a mink Stetson. This year, his Stetson matched his white linen suit, white silk shirt, and white silk tie. His beard was glossy and was barbered with care.

Amarillo Slim Preston specializes in another kind of chic. He is tall, long-faced, and startlingly thin — someone once called him "the advance man for a famine" — and he dresses in a kind of cowboy baroque. His suit was bilious yellow with brown suede shoulders and trimming; on the sides of his lizardskin boots were the letters

SLIM in white leather; the crown of his Stetson was encircled by a rattlesnake's skin, the creature's mouth gaping forward toward the brim, its rattle vertical on one side, like a feather.

None of the others even tried to compete with Addington or Slim, although several had chosen a part and were dressed for it. Gene Fisher, another amateur from Texas, wore a battered Stetson and a scarlet United States Cavalry shirt, buttoned diagonally from waist to shoulder. With his silver hair and full, silver mustache, he looked like a reincarnation of Kit Carson. One young cowboy was wearing a bright blue Stetson and a black shirt embroidered with black silk curlicues. Ken Smith, who is also a chess master and was Bobby Fischer's second in the Reykjavík marathon with Boris Spassky, wore what he always wears at competitions — a frock coat and a decrepit top hat, which he claims was found in the Ford Theatre the night Lincoln was assassinated. Smith has a ragged beard, a squeaky voice, and a girth like that of Swinburne's giant slumbering boar: "the blind bulk of the immeasurable beast." Each time he wins a pot, he lumbers to his feet, doffs his topper to the audience, and pipes, "What a player!"

The others were less fashion-conscious, although, like the oysters in *Through the Looking-Glass,* "Their coats were brushed, their faces washed, / Their shoes were clean and neat." Brunson and Straus wore pale blue suede jackets over navy blue shirts and trousers. Chip Reese had abandoned his velour track suits and reverted to his Ivy League origins: gray flannel trousers and a gray shirt with blue pinstripes. Bobby Baldwin was dressed in gray trousers and a gray Lacoste tennis shirt, at once sporting and sober, to suit his image. Even Mickey Appleman was wearing a neat beige corduroy jacket over his black T-shirt, and Stu Ungar wore a clean bowling shirt.

As the tournament organizer, Eric Drache seated the seventy-five players at eight tables by mixing their names in a plastic bowl and drawing lots. They took their places slowly as he called their names, joking nervously among themselves about the unfairness of the draw, the relative strength of each table, their own lack of form. The spectators jostled for position at the rails, the lights blazed, the cameras whirred, the monotonous voice of the switchboard operator over the intercom — "Telephone call for Jack Binion," or "Telephone call for Eric Drache" — was temporarily stilled.

Jack Binion climbed onto a chair at the back of the room, directly under the banner announcing BINION'S HORSESHOE PRESENTS THE WORLD SERIES OF POKER 1981. He beamed down on the crowd, looking dignified in a three-piece gray flannel suit and a free but discreet variation of the Old Etonian tie. He motioned for quiet, did not get it, then introduced the players over the babble of the casino: name, place of origin, a word or so of praise. His favorite description was "plenty tough." The players rose in turn from their seats, glanced furtively at the audience, avoided looking at the cameras, and sat down again quickly. The railbirds applauded each one — the local heroes enthusiastically, the rest politely.

There was a noisy pause, and then Frank Cutrona, the floor manager, and his assistants bustled around the tables distributing ten-thousand-dollar racks of chips. Another pause while the players counted them and arranged them on the baize, each according to his own private architectural plan: neatly by colors or mixed in apparently haphazard ways; in tens, in twenties, in tall unstable-looking towers of yellow-and-green twenty-fives, black hundreds, gray five hundreds. The dealers pulled back their cuffs to display the gold at their wrists, fanned out each pack of cards in an arc to check that it was complete, flipped it over face down, mixed it flat on the table, according to the Vegas formula, shuffled, cut, and began to deal. The crowd behind the rails craned solemnly forward, chomping gum, like cows at a gate.

*   *   *

The first player was eliminated an hour and a half later. There was a brief rattle of applause as he got to his feet and nodded to his companions at the table. He looked sheepish. Ten thousand dollars is a great deal of money to spend on ninety minutes' entertainment. "Hunnerd an' eleven bucks a minute," muttered someone in the crowd, adding pedantically, "More or less."

By the time play stopped for early dinner, at five-thirty, fourteen more had gone, including several of the "plenty tough" players who had made it to the final table in other tournaments: Milo Jacobson, who lost to Brunson in the 1977 final; Charlie Dunwoody, fifth placed in 1980; the actor Gabe Kaplan, sixth placed in 1980 and winner of the 1979 Poker Classic in Reno; Bones Berland, a formidable young player who was runner-up in 1977.

For the first time, the conversation in the Sombrero Room was muted, and the wives and girlfriends seemed, also for the first time, to have a role to play — listening and shaking their heads while their men muttered to them about bad draws and dead cards. Johnny and Virgie Moss sat together in a far corner, heads close, her hand consolingly over his, like young marrieds. Near them, Louise Brunson watched anxiously while Doyle demolished a double helping of chocolate cake. Jack Straus, his mouth drawn down at the corners, sat hunched over a cup of coffee with his son and Larry. For the tournament, he had drawn a seat at a table with an elderly woman with red-dyed hair and more diamonds than Harry Winston's shopwindow: diamonds at her throat and bosom, diamonds around both wrists, diamonds on every finger. Not only was she an amateur; she had only recently started to play hold 'em. But all day she had been hitting card after miracle card, and no one at the table could contain her. Straus's stack was already down to $2000, and his mood was black. "If he loses to her, he'll be in a bad temper for a year," his son said.

* * *

All poker is a form of social Darwinism: the fit survive, the weak go broke. Walter Matthau once said, "The game exemplifies the worst aspects of capitalism that have made our country so great." Since Las Vegas provides continuous action at the highest level and for the highest stakes, most of the fittest eventually find their way there and discover, with startling rapidity, whether or not they really are survivors. "It's like an experiment in evolution in which you have speeded up time," said David Sklansky. But in freeze-out no-limit poker, where there are no second chances and any mistake may be terminal, the evolutionary process is not only accelerated but also distorted. Because in the early stages luck plays as large a part as skill, the professionals know they are at a disadvantage, and only the amateurs, who have nothing to lose but their stakes, seem to enjoy themselves. All month, the World Series had been building to this grand climax, but now, when play resumed, the atmosphere was gloomy, the expressions were morose, the play was monotonous.

The professionals continued to fall: Johnny Moss, Junior Whited, and Tony Salinas, the big Texan who had been formally sentenced to five years in Vegas. Betty Carey was eliminated at eight fifteen; Barbara Freer, the other top woman contender, a couple of hours later.

The previous day, I had talked to Barbara Freer, a very small middle-aged woman with a very large pompadour of dark hair, who has played in the big event since 1978. "When I sat down that first time, I'd never played hold 'em in my life," she told me. "But I figured as long as it was cards I'd learn as I went along. There were fifty-four entrants that year and, believe it or not, I finished eighteenth." She has bright eyes and the pugnacious confidence of a classy flyweight.

"I believe it," I said.

She nodded contentedly. "I prefer playing with men," she said. "Women tend to be petty — if you beat them, they tell you you were lucky. With men, the aggression is straightforward, and I love it. Instead of frightening me, it goads me on. I have a great desire to win, and I love the competition. One of these days, I'm going to be up there in Binion's Hall of Fame with the other poker greats."

At ten thirty the next evening — she was the last player to be eliminated on the first day — she shrugged dismissively when I asked her what happened. "I had two pairs against his trips," she said. "But I had to be there. I'm a gambler, right?" Her voice was still jaunty, but the contagious confidence had leaked away and her large, painted mouth was unsteady. She looked like someone who has been dealt a mortal blow yet is still, in a confused way, ambulatory. It was a look I came to recognize as the big names were knocked out.

"What makes the heroic?" asked Nietzsche, and answered himself, "To go to meet simultaneously one's greatest sorrow and one's greatest hope." He also wrote, "Timid, ashamed, awkward, like a tiger whose leap has failed: this is how I have often seen you slink aside, you higher men. A throw you made had failed. But what of that, you dice-throwers! . . . If great things you attempted have turned out failures, does that mean you yourselves are — failures?" For the brief period in which the losers came to terms with the fact that their chances of becoming World Champion were over for another year, the answer was unequivocal. "Hell," said the crestfallen cowboy in the black shirt embroidered with black silk curlicues, "they beat me like an ugly stepchild."

All the next day, the mayhem continued: Jack Straus, Puggy Pearson, Amarillo Slim, Jesse Alto. Straus, in fact, was out within half an hour of the resumption of play. "There was twenty-eight thousand in the pot," he said. "I moved all in with my chips, turned over my cards, and told him I had him beat. Which was true. But he stayed in anyway and outdrew me on Fifth Street." His eyes were not quite focused, and the expression on his face, like that of all the others who wandered into the Sombrero Room one by one, was stricken.

Only Johnny Moss allowed his anger to show through. He was standing near the reception desk, by a little trestle table on which were spread copies of his authorized biography, published by himself: *Champion of Champions: A Portrait of the Greatest Poker Player of Our Time.* The price was $15, and trade seemed to be brisk. Virgie Moss sat dourly behind the table, a cigar box full of money at her elbow. Moss jabbed a finger meaningfully at the title and reminded me that he had already won the high-low split competition this year, despite his age. "But I ain't a-enterin' the champeenship next year. Nine-handed is too many. Seven-handed, like we played it in Texas, that's how it should be. Nine-handed you gotta sit there and wait for the nuts to break the suckers. I don' wanna play with suckers, I wanna play with gamblers. With gamblers, you play a fi-i-ine edge, not the nuts." He glared truculently down at his wife. "Ain't that right, baby?" he said.

Her leathery face creased in an indulgent, youthful smile. "Sure is, honeycakes."

The game droned on uneventfully through the second afternoon until around four o'clock, when a young player called Ricky Clayton suddenly slumped sidewise and forward across the table, like a puppet whose strings have snapped. As the television cameras zoomed in, Eric Drache bustled up, hands raised as though in surrender. "O.K., O.K., no trouble," he said. "Just stomach cramps. It's happened before. Let's break for an early dinner."

An hour later, Ricky Clayton was back in his seat, moving his chips around as if nothing had happened.

Not long before play ended for the day, when only twenty of the seventy-five starters were left, a big hand began to build between Chip Reese and a surly Texan, Bill Smith. Smith's face is pitted and blunt-featured, like Karl Malden's, and, almost alone among the serious poker players, he not only drinks while he plays but also seems drunk; he weaves a little in his seat, checking and raising in a thick voice. The cocktail waitresses keep the glass of whiskey at his elbow permanently freshened. But he is what Jack Binion calls a "plenty tough" player, dangerous and aggressive, and the other contestants treat him warily. This time, however, when he came out betting, Reese raised him $8000. Smith stared at him sullenly while the gamblers who were no longer playing crowded around the table.

"If Bill calls, ol' Chip's gonna have to swim in the lake," Johnny Moss murmured contentedly.

Smith sipped his whiskey thoughtfully, and then took four gray chips from a stack of twenty and pushed the rest in. He seemed utterly unconcerned, as though he were playing for pennies. The dealer cleared his throat, hitched back his shirt cuffs, burned the top card, and dealt the flop: a jack and a seven of diamonds, and a three of clubs. Reese considered the cards stonily and bet $20,000. Without hesitating, Smith put both hands behind his stack of chips and pushed them all into the center.

The dealer counted them and said, "Raise nineteen three." A faint murmur came from the railbirds — a low, solemn sound, like keening.

Reese sat very still for a time, and then called the bet grimly, leaving himself with less than $10,000. There was now about $75,000 in the middle of the table.

With Smith all in, there could be no more betting, so both players turned over their hole cards: Reese had two jacks, giving him three of a kind with the communal jack exposed; Smith had an eight and ten of diamonds, giving him four cards to a flush and what is called a gut-shot draw to both a straight and a straight flush.

The dealer burned the top card and turned the king of spades, which helped neither player. Then he paused dramatically, like an actor who knows the audience is hanging on each gesture, burned another card, and turned over a five of diamonds. Smith had made his flush.

Reaching forward unsteadily, he dragged the mountain of chips toward him while Reese watched, mouth drawn tight, eyes pained and astonished.

*　*　*

On May 20, the third day of the championship, the front pages of the local papers were divided equally between a running story about a duck with an arrow through its breast and the election for control of the local culinary union. The duck had been nimble enough to avoid its well-wishers for several days, although the arrow stuck out on each side of it like a clothes hanger. The new secretary of the culinary union, who had been elected on a reformist ticket despite alleged opposition from the mob, seemed likely to need a similar charmed life. "No," he announced at his victory press conference. "I haven't received any death threats. Yet."

There were now twenty players left in the event, with three quarters of a million dollars' worth of chips shared among them. The leader, with $81,600, was Perry Green, a tiny, bearded dumpling of a man, who looks like a miniature Henry VIII but is in fact a fur trader from Anchorage and a devout Orthodox Jew. Chip Reese trailed the field, with $7800.

Doyle Brunson, in sixth place, with $47,800, seemed uneasy and depressed. "It's been uphill all the way so far," he said. "Just cain't seem to hit a card." He was suffering from toothache and moved in an aura of myrrh.

The one cheerful face in the pervading gloom belonged to Andy Moore, the only surviving outsider in the tournament. Moore is in his midthirties and is raffish-looking. He owns a bar in Sarasota, Florida, where he plays poker twice a week in a small social game, like thousands of others around the country: two-dollar ante, pot limit, win or lose two or three hundred dollars. "Mostly I lose," he told me. "My friend here" — a tall, ebullient man, who seemed as elated as Moore by Moore's success — "he just beats me like a drum." The tall friend laughed and slapped Moore's shoulder, then mine: all pals together. "I could play more often if I wanted," Moore continued. "But I've got all the other bad habits in life, too, so I just can't seem to find the time. I like girls and drinking and golf too much, I guess." The friend laughed knowingly and slapped him on the shoulder again.

In 1977, Moore moved out to Las Vegas to try the gambling life, but left after three months with the money he had come with, having lost at poker and won at golf. "I love the excitement of gambling, but the coldness of this town leaves a lot to be desired," he said. "I've lived in Sarasota for twenty-five years — went to high school there — and although it's grown from maybe twenty-five thousand to a hundred thousand in that time, it's still a fairly small town. It's warm, it's friendly, people know each other, the atmosphere is good. For me, Vegas is like a block of ice. Even if I won the championship, I wouldn't want to come back to this cold life again."

Meanwhile, he was living out a fairy story. The night before the championship, he and his friend had put up $500 each for him to play nine other players for the ten-thousand-dollar stake to enter the big event. He won, and by the end of the first day he had parlayed his winnings up to $45,000, which placed him third. Since then, his money had sunk considerably — to $12,900 at the start of Day Three — but that only added to the excitement. "The point is, it's only cost me five hundred," he said. "It's not like I'm blowing ten thousand and trying to protect it. I'm here on a million-to-one shot, and if it hits, it hits."

Unlike the other players, Moore made no attempt to conceal his pleasure, and he wanted the whole world to share it. Each hand he played, he held the cards up for the railbirds to see. They loved him for that and because he was the underdog. Whenever he won, they applauded loudly, and he twisted around in his chair, beaming at them and shaking his head disbelievingly. When he lost, his loose mouth drooped and his back curved despondently. "Tough!" cried the railbirds, and "Keep after 'em, Andy!"

The gigantic Ken Smith, the chess master, was also playing to the crowd, not only doffing his top hat and bleating "What a player!" but also using the crowd as a sounding board whenever he decided to coffeehouse — or bluff verbally — an opponent. Early in the afternoon, he found himself head to head with a morose-looking man named Don Furrh. As soon as Smith bet, Furrh's hands moved ominously to the back of his chips. Then they hovered while he considered whether or not to move all in.

"I've got a real hand here," Smith squeaked. "You gotta be strong, Don."

A large bleached blonde in cut-off Levi's and a halter shouted from the rail, "You tell him, Smitty!"

Ken Smith's voice rose another decibel. "It's a real good hand I'm holding here."

"Amen!" called the blonde.

Furrh stared contemptuously at Smith, shrugged, and threw in his cards. But the next deal, as though primed and goaded by Smith's performance, he moved all in with a jack and a nine when a jack fell on the flop. He had chosen the wrong moment and the wrong opponent: Jay

Heimowitz, one of the few Easterners who can face the Texans as an equal at hold 'em. Heimowitz called Furrh's bet without even pausing, and turned over his hole cards disdainfully: two jacks. Exit Furrh.

Minutes later, Ken Smith was at it again, his "What a player!" almost drowning out the din of the slot machines. Doyle Brunson, who has known Smith for thirty years, grinned at him benevolently. "You're all heart, Ken," he said. "Heart and belly." The railbirds applauded. "You know what I'm gonna do?" Brunson continued. "I'm gonna raise you on two rags and bluff you right out."

"Try me," piped Smith, and he came out betting when the next flop was dealt: king, queen, jack.

"Raise!" said Brunson so loudly that his jowls quivered. He put both hands behind his now depleted stacks of chips and pushed them belligerently into the center. Smith paused, shrugged, and docilely folded. Brunson pulled in the pot, then turned over his hole cards and tossed them, face up, across the table: a six and a five of different suits. He rose majestically to his feet, doffed his Stetson, and cried, basso profundo, "What a player!" The crowd roared.

Although Brunson appeared to be enjoying himself, the cards were running steadily against him. He told me later that the only good hand he had been dealt in three days was a pair of kings, and those he had thrown away when Gene Fisher — Kit Carson revisited — reraised him with what Brunson assumed, correctly, to be three nines. "I never even had a draw to a straight or a flush," he said. "Every time I won a pot, it was with the worst hand." It is an indication of his supreme skill that, despite this, he came in eleventh out of seventy-five players. But little by little his chips were whittled away, and in the middle of the third day he and Andy Moore, each now desperately short of chips, both went all in before the flop. Moore held an ace and a four of spades, Brunson a king and a two of diamonds. The flop helped neither of them, but an ace fell on Fourth Street, and that was the end of Brunson's tournament. The crowd applauded him vigorously, and he replied with an expansive wave of his arm, like visiting royalty. But his eyes were vague, and his mobile face seemed battered.

A couple of hours earlier, the poker players had briefly lost their poker faces when there were still fifteen of them left and Eric Drache announced that the three remaining tables would be amalgamated into two. The seats would be allocated, Drache said, by drawing cards: red for Table One, black for Table Two, one to eight of each color for the seat numbers. Frank, the floor manager, shuffled and dealt while Drache called out the players' names. Suddenly, everybody began protesting at once: the first four cards dealt were all red. Someone shouted "It's a fix!" and the rest chimed in, demanding a new deal. Patiently, Frank gathered in the cards, shuffled, and dealt again: ace, two, three of clubs.

"Ain't possible!" cried Stu Ungar. "It's five thousand to one against!"

"I don't care if it's five million to one," Frank replied. "That's how the cards came and that's how the seating stays."

"Right," said Drache.

"Right," said Jack Binion, the final authority.

The players moved reluctantly to their new places, muttering to one another darkly. Their problem was not cards but superstition; even the losers were obscurely afraid of what a new seat at a new table might do to them.

Soon after the change, two retired farmers were eliminated: Sam Moon, an elderly stick of a man from Corpus Christi, Texas, who raises tomatoes and plays regularly in all the tournaments, and Milton Butts, whose sister and brother-in-law sat behind him all day long, living each hand with him. Butts wore a cheap blue nylon shirt, a baseball cap, and thick glasses. He has very large hands and no teeth, and he looked, like Moon, as if he would have been more at home in *The Grapes of Wrath* than in a high-stakes poker game. When Butts lost his last chips, his sister hugged him and wept.

Of the three New Yorkers left, Mickey Appleman went first, rising blank-faced from the table, seemingly unable to speak: Harpo playing King Lear. He disappeared into his room and did not emerge for several hours. Jay Heimowitz, however, was playing with ominous authority, as if he had decided that this, finally, was his year. In comparison, Stu Ungar, the wonder boy who had been the surprise winner the previous year, was living by his wits, ducking and weaving and counterpunching but avoiding any big confrontation.

In contrast, Bill Smith, who continued to confound all the rules by drinking and winning, lost $37,000 to a tough-looking professional named Sam Petrillo, then came out raising on the very next hand, which he won. Soon after that, Stu Ungar moved all in against him with two aces in the hole and a full house on the flop. Again, Smith lost heavily, but still his aggression did not waver. By the end of the day, he seemed very drunk yet was in second place, with $114,800 — only $13,500 less than the leader, Bobby Baldwin. "If Bill ends up beating all the nice guys, like Bobby, it's going to set the image of poker back ten years," one of the professionals muttered.

That evening, gold bracelets were distributed to those who had already won the other events, and Bill Boyd was formally inducted into the Poker Hall of Fame, alongside Edmond Hoyle, Wild Bill Hickok (shot holding two pairs, aces and eights, thereafter known as Dead Man's Hand), Sid Wyman, Nick the Greek Dandalos, Red Winn, Blondie Forbes, and Johnny Moss. Bill Boyd is a sober-suited, gentle old man who looks like a family doctor and manages the card room at the Golden Nugget. He is also the undefeated champion at five-card stud — so good that in the end no one would play against him, and the event lapsed from the World Series.

When all the prizes had been given and the formalities were done, Benny Binion finally spoke. To thunderous applause, he ambled up to the microphone, beamed vaguely around the packed room, and drawled, "I hope you all get out of here a winner." End of speech. More thunderous applause.

11

HALF an hour before play ended on the third night, Andy Moore, everyone's favorite underdog, raised unwisely with a pair of aces and a pair of queens and was trapped by Gene Fisher, the impassive Texan, who had made a straight on the flop. That mistake cost Moore $20,000 and also his equilibrium; he lost two more pots immediately afterward, both by narrow margins, and ended the day trailing the field, with $27,000. When play began on the last day, his eyes were puffy and he still seemed upset. "It was a hand I didn't have to play," he said. "I kept cussing myself for it all night."

Even so, I said, out of seventy-five starters he had made

it to the last nine, and, whatever happened now, he would walk away with at least $15,000 in prize money.

"And it only cost you five hundred bucks," said his tall friend cheerfully. But Moore was not to be consoled.

Chicago Sam Petrillo was the first to fall. Petrillo is a local of ten years' standing, a hard, sullen man with thick lips and a thin cigar. He gets his nickname from the town where he left a wife and three children in order to become a professional poker player. In Vegas, he started out dealing blackjack but now plays poker twelve hours a day six days a week. Twenty minutes after play began, he moved all in with an ace and a king in the hole and was called by Bobby Baldwin, who was holding two queens. The queens were good, and Baldwin won a pot of $150,000, bringing his total as leader to $200,000.

Ten minutes later, Baldwin was dealt the queens again, and this time his victim was Andy Moore. Moore pocketed his prize money and grinned at the crowd for the last time. All he said was "I'd have liked to have lasted longer."

Often in poker games, certain hands keep recurring and seem unbeatable. Doyle Brunson, for example, twice won the World Championship holding a ten and a deuce — a hand that in an ordinary game would be virtually unplayable. But both times Brunson was forced to see the flop, despite his better judgment, because the antes in the closing stages of the tournament were so high — $4000 from each player and a blind opening bet of $8000 — that he was partly committed before any other cards were turned. On both occasions, the communal cards gave him a full house of three tens and two deuces. This year, it seemed as if two queens might be the magic hand. Seventy minutes after Baldwin disposed of Andy Moore with them, he found himself head to head with Perry Green, but this time it was Green who was holding the pair of queens. Baldwin had two nines in the hole, and a third nine was turned on the flop. When Green bet $42,000, Baldwin, lips primly pursed, raised $85,000, to set Green in for all his money. Green sat immobile, scarcely breathing, like a tubby Buddha. He had kicked his shoes off when he first sat down, and his socked feet were pressed neatly together; his round belly was creased by the table; his plump arms encircled his stacks of chips; his hands were crossed demurely over his cards. He stared at Baldwin for two full minutes, then pushed the rest of his chips into the center. The dealer turned a jack, then a third queen, to match Green's pair. The crowd sighed in unison. Someone shouted, "Hang in there, Bobby!" As the dealer pushed the two-hundred-twenty-thousand-dollar mountain toward Green, Baldwin tried to smile, but the muscles around his mouth seemed unable to cope with the effort.

An hour before, Baldwin had seemed set to win his second title, but now the stricken look was on his face, and he began to push his luck in a desperate attempt to recoup. But at this level the players are alert to every nuance. They knew that Baldwin winning was different from Baldwin wounded, and they moved in for the kill. Three times, he tried to bluff, and each time he was called, the last time for a huge sum by Stu Ungar, who had made the fatal two queens on the flop. Fifteen minutes later, Baldwin was dealt two kings and moved all in against Gene Fisher. But Fisher had the magic two queens in the hole, and once again the third queen was turned, this time on Fifth Street. This time Baldwin did manage a smile as he made his way out through the applauding crowd. His wife followed him, touching his back reassuringly with her fingertips.

While Baldwin was playing, the outcome of the championship had seemed almost certain. His departure threw the whole event off balance. Of the six players now left, only Ungar had won the title before, but he was so young that the railbirds still considered his defeat of Brunson the previous year a lucky fluke.

"It's up for grabs," said a wizened old man in a Hawaiian shirt. "First come, first served."

"Keep it in Texas!" called a tall cowboy crushed in behind him.

Ken Smith raised his topper in acknowledgment. And for a period the contest seemed to become a question more of places than of personalities, hold 'em being, by tradition, a Texas game. Brunson, in fact, had made a large patriotic bet with Gabe Kaplan that the Texans would beat the Jews. Now the forces were equally matched: Ken Smith, Gene Fisher, and Bill Smith against Stu Ungar, Perry Green, and Jay Heimowitz.

At the start of the day, Heimowitz had been in third place, with $103,000, but now he was down to less than $50,000. He is a tall, rangy businessman from Monticello, New York, with a powerful nose and chin and with the build and temperament of an athlete. That morning, he had been up at six, had run a couple of miles while the air was still cool, and had done "a few hundred" leg lifts and other exercises; then he had gone back to bed until it was time to play. At each meal break, he disappeared into his room to shower and shave. "Feeling good and trying to look good can make you play better," he said. During the game, he moved about quite a bit, standing, stretching, pacing around the table, although the impression he created was not one of restlessness but one of intense energy carefully restrained. Of all the players, he seems the most obviously dedicated, the most powerfully driven by the need to excel. "Desire," he said. "That's what distinguishes the top players from the rest — the strong competitive will to win. A lot of people can play well for short periods, but after a couple of hours and one bad beat their game blows up. You have to be able to sit there and strive for hour after hour. You must accept a bad turn of the cards, or no cards, or being outdrawn unjustly, and you must overcome all that mentally. You don't have to be the best player to win, but you can beat the best by will power, by doing continually what you're supposed to do to the very limit of your ability. Poker is like everything else in this life: almost any goal is attainable, and the only time you fail is when you give up."

But on this final day will power and discipline were not enough to overcome the huge antes and a series of second-best hands. Finally, at four thirty, Heimowitz was dealt the miracle two queens. He bet heavily and was called only by Ungar. The flop was king, jack, ten of different suits, giving him an open-ended straight to go with his pair of queens. Although it was a powerful hand, he thought a long time before calling when Ungar made a bet large enough to set him in for all his remaining chips. Since there could be no more betting, Heimowitz turned over his queens. Ungar paused, grinned, twitched, and flipped over his hole cards: two jacks, giving him, with the flop, a set of three. Heimowitz got up abruptly, clasped his hands and flexed his shoulders in some obscure isometric ritual, and gripped the back of his chair fiercely, as though about to perform a feat of strength.

His face was solemn. The room was silent, except for the permanent whir of the air conditioning. The dealer burned the top card and turned over a seven, burned another card and turned over the fourth jack. For the first time that day, the queens had failed to perform their magic. Heimowitz left looking grim, despite his prize money — $30,000.

The very next hand, Ungar broke Bill Smith when he flopped a flush against Smith's pair of sixes and straight draw. Smith finished his drink, pocketed $37,500 in crisp hundred-dollar bills, and weaved his way out. The crowd applauded him loudly but with a certain sense of relief. The new, clean-living image of poker had been spared for another year.

When the game broke for early dinner, at five, only four players were left. Stu Ungar, who two hours before had been trailing the field with $50,000, was the clear leader, with $340,000; Perry Green was second, with $220,000; the two Texans, Gene Fisher and Ken Smith, had $95,000 each. Brunson shook his jowls. "That bet of mine with Gabe don't look too healthy," he said.

It looked even less healthy a couple of hours later, when Perry Green eliminated Ken Smith with four aces against a top-straight draw. Smith lumbered to his feet and raised his topper when Jack Binion handed him his prize money. Someone in the crowd shouted, "What a player!" Smith doffed his hat again.

At that point, Green seemed impregnable. He sat neatly at the table, gathered into himself behind a four-hundred-thousand-dollar mountain, like a man at absolute zero, every molecule of his body unmoving. Perched on his head was a white peaked cap emblazoned with the Horseshoe's insignia. His eyes, under its shadow, were unblinking. In comparison, Stu Ungar looked as if he had been broken and thrown carelessly into his chair — as vulnerable and helpless as an ungainly fledgling fallen from its nest. He squirmed about, arms unstrung, head peering this way and that, simian jaw and thin fingers working restlessly.

When Ungar won the World Championship at his first attempt, in 1980, beating Doyle Brunson in the final against every prediction, he had been playing hold 'em for only a few months. He was twenty-six at the time, and had come to Las Vegas from New York with the reputation of being the world's best gin rummy player — so good that he could no longer find anyone willing to play him, even in the Borscht Belt, where he had been beating all comers since he was twelve years old. His father was a bookmaker, and young Stu grew up in the cardplaying, gambling environment known as "New York goulash." When Eric Drache ran his own poker game in New Jersey, Ungar used to play in it with considerable success, although he was only fifteen. Drache used to call him, fondly, "the idiot savant." His IQ was rumored to be 185, but he seemed to have used it only to play cards and calculate odds. According to Drache, Ungar hadn't had a bank account until he came out to Las Vegas, and when he was finally persuaded to open one he thought he had to go to the bank each time he wrote a check. "Yet he is unbelievably sharp, wholly conscious of everything that's going on," said Drache. "I'd hate to try to cheat on him with his wife — if he had a wife. He'd know instantly." He also has, it is universally agreed, an unlimited natural talent for cards. His poker record in Vegas is said to be even better than Chip Reese's: a couple of million, probably more, in less than two years, I was told — "although it's hard to clock him, because he's in and out of the money all the time, winning it at cards, throwing it away again on the sports or craps or any proposition that catches his fancy." Jack Straus calls him, admiringly, the Kamikaze Kid. Drache puts it more primly. "He has some very bad habits," he says. But apparently Vegas, for once, is not to blame for them; it is rumored that when his father died, long before young Stu came out to Nevada, he blew his whole legacy — $90,000 — in two weeks at the racetrack.

Yet, despite his natural gifts, when the tournament began the bookmakers gave him only a forty-to-one chance of winning the championship for the second time, and Ungar agreed with them: he bet heavily on Brunson, not at all on himself.

Even when it came down to the last three, he seemed unlikely to win, although Gene Fisher, still looking like the noble frontiersman, with his bright blue eyes, his drooping mustache, and his silver hair curling under the rim of his battered Stetson, was now too low on chips to be a threat. In contrast, the immobile Perry Green seemed as unforgiving as a rock wall. Johnny Moss, however, was not impressed. "I reckon Stuey's got it made," he said. "He may not look like no Buffalo Bill, but he's one tough poker player. That boy's got alligator blood in his veins." For Moss, there is no greater compliment he can pay a fellow gambler.

Twenty minutes after Bill Smith was broken, a big pot began to build between Green and Ungar. Green, holding an ace of spades and a queen of diamonds, bet modestly, and called when Ungar, with a pair of kings in the hole, raised $10,000. The cameramen closed in as the dealer turned the first three cards: an ace of clubs and a ten

and five of diamonds. Ungar glanced at the cards dis-
consolately, flopped sidewise in his seat, and tapped the
baize twice with his forefinger to check. Green stared at
him and then at the three innocent cards. Only his eye-
balls moved. Carefully, he separated several towers of
chips from the bastion in front of him and pushed them
toward the center. The dealer counted them expertly and
said, "Sixty thousand." Ungar lolled over still farther in
his seat, until he seemed in danger of falling on the floor.
He knew that when Green bet so much — twice the
amount in the pot — he was saying two things: first, that
he himself had a good hand and wanted to win the pot
right there, without further hassle; second, that he recognized that Ungar, too, held powerful cards — probably
two big diamonds — and wanted to offer him the worst
possible odds for making his hand. Ungar took a few
chips from his stacks and began to dance them through
his fingers, up and down, in and out, like a juggler. Then,
quickly, as though not to give himself time to change his
mind, he separated the sixty thousand from his now
diminished pile and pushed them forward. The dealer
gathered them in, counted them, burned the top card,
and dealt the king of hearts, making Ungar three kings.
Ungar straightened in his chair, shook his head im-
patiently, as if in answer to some private question, put
his hands casually behind his remaining chips, and
pushed them into the center. There was silence while the
dealer counted. "Ninety thousand," he said, at last. A
voice from the crowd said "Wow!" Silence fell again while
Perry Green sat, seemingly interminably, weighing Ungar's move. One minute, two minutes, three minutes.
Finally, he separated nine stacks of twenty gray chips
from the rest of his money and shoved them in. The

dealer dealt a four of clubs, and the crowd erupted. Green blinked once and did not move. The pot was $330,000.

For the second time in the event, Ungar had moved into the lead, with $400,000 to Green's $300,000; Gene Fisher limped behind with $50,000. A quarter of an hour later, he was out, unluckily, when Perry Green made a flush on Fifth Street to beat his three kings. Fisher rose slowly, tilted his handsome head to the applauding crowd, and grinned like a schoolboy when Binion handed him the third prize — $75,000.

Brunson, standing with Gabe Kaplan behind one of the television cameramen, fished his bankroll from his voluminous trousers and began counting out hundred-dollar bills. "So much for the Texans," said Kaplan. "We got ourselves an all-Jewish final."

The win against Fisher gave Green a hundred-thousand-dollar pot, putting him in the lead once more. There was now three quarters of a million dollars' worth of chips on the table, shared between an Orthodox Jewish furrier from Alaska and a twenty-seven-year-old wonder boy from New York. Yet such is the nature of freeze-out poker that the money would have no meaning until the last pot was won. The chips were like rapiers in a fencing match — instruments to attack, parry, counterthrust until one or the other of the duelists delivered the coup de grâce. It was the final, purest expression of the high rollers' attitude toward money, "the language of poker," with which they can express every subtle nuance of meaning but which otherwise has no significance until the game is over.

After the departure of Gene Fisher, the antes were raised to $4000, the blind opening bet to $8000, forcing both the finalists to play on the slimmest of chances.

Despite this, the game was subdued, almost static, for half an hour, as each of them probed for a weakness and withdrew quickly at the first sign of confrontation. Then, at eight thirty, when Green was still comfortably ahead, a gigantic pot developed after a jack of diamonds and a nine and eight of clubs were turned on the flop. Ungar, who was holding an ace and jack of clubs, moved all in with two jacks and four cards to the top club flush. Green, with a ten and deuce of clubs, saw the bet, giving him a draw to an open-ended straight and also a draw to what was in fact a weaker flush. The fourth card was a third jack, the fifth card a six of spades. The pot was worth $560,000, and it put Ungar firmly in the lead, with $600,000 to Green's $150,000.

At that point, Green's whole manner changed. Although he remained as impassive as ever, moving hardly at all, his face registering nothing, his aura of threat and imperturbability seemed to leak slowly away, as if through a very small puncture. It was as if the possibility of actually winning the championship had not been quite what he intended when he entered, and now that he had come so far the prospect was too much for him.

"It's all over," Straus said. "The kid's gonna eat him up like a boarding-house pie."

But it was not until nine forty-five, after another hour and a quarter of desultory, gloomy play, that the end came. Ungar, with the ace and queen of hearts in the hole, made a large bet before the flop; Green, holding a ten of clubs and a nine of diamonds, called it guardedly. The flop was a seven of diamonds and an eight and four of hearts, giving Ungar four hearts and Green an open-ended straight draw. When Ungar bet again, Green moved in with all his remaining chips. They sat as they had sat for hours, Green with his round belly pressed against the table and his plump hands folded neatly over his cards, Ungar lolling sidewise with his left arm flung back over his chair, fractionally raising and lowering his cards with the bony fingers of his right hand. He paused a long time before calling the bet, and then both men turned over their cards. Green stared at Ungar's two hearts, nodded once, and shifted his eyes back to the communal cards in the center. Ungar's long mouth twitched, and he fidgeted uneasily in his chair. "For a while, it looked pretty dim out there," he said later.

The rustling, whirring calm that passes for silence in Binion's Horseshoe thickened, like the air before a thunderstorm. The dealer burned the top card and turned over the four of clubs, burned the next card and turned over the queen of diamonds. For the last time in the tournament, the queens had worked their magic. Green had not filled his straight, and Ungar had won his second title with a pair of queens, a pair of fours, and an ace kicker. They had been head to head for one and three-quarters hours.

"Hey!" said Ungar, and jumped galvanically in his chair as the storm broke around him. The spectators were clapping and shouting their approval, the television cameras zoomed in and out — on Ungar, on Green, on the huge mounds of chips, and on the cards lying where they had been dealt. From the other end of the casino came a concerted rattle, as if the slot machines themselves were applauding. Grinning from jug ear to jug ear, Jack Binion bustled forward, followed by two security guards carrying bundles of money, which they heaped prodigally, like firewood, on the table. Binion clasped Ungar and Green to him, his arms around their shoulders, while a barrage of cameras flashed. Someone stuck a microphone in front of Ungar, but all he could manage was "Great!"

For the last time that year, Jack Binion divided up the prize money: $375,000 to Stu Ungar, $150,000 to Perry Green, in packets of fifty hundred-dollar bills, ten packets to a bundle. The television cameras probed lovingly around it. The security guards watched them grimly.

*　　*　　*

Afterward, there was a confused and largely inaudible press conference in the annex to the Sombrero Room. Someone asked Ungar how old he had been when he started gambling.

He ducked his head and muttered, "Seven or eight, sumtin' like that."

Someone else asked what he did in his spare time.

"Spare time?" Ungar cocked his head and eyed the journalist incredulously. "Only time I'm not gamblin' is when I'm sleepin' or eatin'." He seemed more restless than ever, shifting about continuously on the hard little chair he had been provided with, shaking his head, scratching himself vaguely.

The inevitable question came: What would he do with all that money?

Ungar ducked his head again, giggled, and muttered into his chest, "Lose it."

"Sorry," said the journalist. "I didn't catch that."

Ungar straightened out momentarily and grinned at the expectant faces. "I'm gonna put it in the bank and give it to my kids, what else?" He let out a brief, uncontrolled gasp of laughter, and the journalists laughed uneasily with him. The transparent skin, stretched corpse-tight across his face, was even paler than usual. He rubbed his eyes, his forehead, the back of his neck, and then stood up suddenly and scratched the small of his back. His grin had gone, and he seemed exhausted. "That's it, fellas," he said.

Perry Green was more ceremonious. He introduced his wife. "Come on over here, Gloria, the gentlemen of the press want to meet you. Now, here she is. Not bad-looking, is she, guys?" He reeled off the names of the staff at his Anchorage headquarters: "I have a wonderful brother who manages the store when I'm gone, along with Grace Black, who manages the store downstairs. And up in the factory I have all those wonderful people — Victor and Mary and Juan and the rest. Without their help, I couldn't come here." He launched into a breathless roll call of the "name celebrities" who had bought his furs: "The Reverend Oral Roberts and Ike and Tina Turner and the Four Freshmen and the Bee Gees and Sam Snead and the owner of the Pittsburgh Pirates . . ."

On the opening day of the tournament, Jack Binion had said to me, "When it's over, talk to the guy who came second. He'll have just won a whole heap of money, but he'll be looking like he's lost everything." Perry Green, however, was bouncing like a rubber ball, as though making up for all those hours of blankness and immobility. "This year, I just accepted the President's award for the Union of Orthodox Congregations," he said. "My daughter's going to become a mother. I'm building a new house for my lovely wife and our five lovely kids. We're establishing an Orthodox synagogue up there in Alaska — the first one — and we want to be within walking distance. Yep, it's been a good year for me."

"And now you've won all this money."

"Yeah, well." His face fell; his tubby little body seemed

to deflate. "I know I disappointed a lot of people," he said. "But I came close, didn't I?"

* * *

By ten o'clock the following morning, the poker tables had been removed from the back of the Horseshoe, along with the banners, the blackboard, and the paraphernalia of the television crews. Workmen in gray dungarees were busy reinstalling the slot machines. The casino was crowded, as usual, with tourists — a sea of sweatshirts and halters, Stetsons and bleached perms. Someone had got hot at one of the craps tables, and the spectators were cheering him on, whooping like Apaches with each new winning roll.

Doyle Brunson was coming out of the Sombrero Room as I arrived. He was dressed in brown, like a Benedictine monk, stately and solemn. "Hell," he said. "I came in eleventh out of seventy-five, so I cain't say it was too disappointing." He patted me genially on the shoulder from his great height, as though in blessing. "But you know and I know that don't make a damn of difference," he went on. "Not to have been at that last table yesterday was the worst thing I can think of. I wasn't miserable, exactly. I just felt empty. All I wanted was to be in there playing." He shrugged, exhaled deeply, sucked in his lower lip, and smiled. "Of all the days of the year, yesterday was the worst. But there ain't nothing I can do now except try to forget it and wait till next year."

In the restaurant, Jack Straus, looking flushed and cheerful, was holding court. He and Betty Carey had been playing all night, and once again Betty was broke. The end had come when an eight, nine, and ten of spades were flopped, then the jack of spades was dealt on Fourth Street. Betty moved all in, and Jack saw her bet. Triumphantly, she turned over the seven of spades and hollered, "Straight flush!" Straus shook his head ruefully. "Wrong end, honey," he said, and turned over the queen of spades.

A journalist from New York was listening to Straus's hectic account of the hand and shaking his head disapprovingly. "Tell me, Mr. Straus," he said primly. "Don't you ever feel sorry for the people you beat?"

Straus stretched comfortably. His left eyelid drooped, and he looked at the journalist's earnest face as though along the barrel of a gun. "Funny you should ask that," he said. He put his elbows on the table. His voice was low and intimate. "Just last month, back in El Paso, I played a house painter and beat him out of his whole month's salary — twelve hundred and forty dollars — and I took him a hundred dollars on tab. When the game was over, he signed his paycheck over to me, and I drove him home to collect the rest. He lived in a lower-middle-class section of town, and when we got to his house his wife was there with their six children. 'Honey,' he said, 'I've got some bad news. I lost the paycheck playing poker.' 'Shush,' she said, and herded the children into the next room. Then she started to cry. 'How're we going to feed the kids next month?' she said. 'Honey,' he said, 'I haven't told you the worst part. I still owe this gentleman a hundred dollars.' Well, while they were talking I was looking around, and I noticed her purse lying open by the telephone. There was a ten-dollar bill in it and a one. So you know what I did?"

As Straus talked, he had gradually leaned forward across the table, until his face was inches from the journalist's. "No," said the journalist, eyes wide with concern. "What did you do?"

Straus's left eye drooped further; his expression was grave. "I just took the ten-dollar bill," he said, "and let him slide for the rest."

*　　*　　*

In 1982, a hundred and four contestants anted up $10,000 each to compete for the thirteenth world hold 'em championship. Doyle Brunson placed fourth, winning $52,000 and bringing his total winnings in the World Series of Poker since its inception, in 1970, to over a million dollars. Jack Straus, having been down to his last $500 on the first day, bluffed his way back from the dead and went on to win the title and $520,000.

INDEX

About the Author

A. Alvarez was born in London in 1929 and educated at Oundle School and Corpus Christi College, Oxford. He has lectured at a number of American universities and has been poetry editor and a regular contributor to *The Observer*, as well as drama critic for *The New Statesman*. He has received the Vachel Lindsay Prize for poetry from *Poetry* (Chicago) and a collection of his verse, *Autumn to Autumn, and Selected Poems 1953–76*, was published in England in 1978.

Mr. Alvarez is also the author of several books of literary criticism, the highly praised *The Savage God: A Study of Suicide, Life After Marriage: Love in an Age of Divorce*, and two novels, *Hers* and *Hunt*. He lives in London with his wife and children, and plays poker every Tuesday.